INVESTIGATING HISTORY

A WORLD STUDY AFTER 1900

Neil DeMarco

Hodder Murray
www.hoddereducation.co.uk

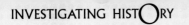
Acknowledgements

The publishers would like to thank the following individuals, institutions and companies for permission to reproduce copyright illustrations in this book:

A & M University: p4; Imperial War Museum: p6, p8, p41, p61 (top); Wellcome Library, London: p11; Mary Evans: p17 (The Woman's Library); p18; p19 (Fawcett Library), p39 (Alexander Meledin), p47, p48; Hulton-Deutsch: p22, Topham Picturepoint: p26, p34; Bildarchiv Preußischer Kulturbesitz: p25; AKG London: p30; David Low, Evening Standard, and for supply of photo Centre for the Study of Cartoons and Caricature, University of Kent, Canterbury, CT2 7NU: p32; David King Collection: p39, p45; Peter Newark's American Pictures: p51; Corbis/Seattle Post-Intelligencer Collection; Museum of History & Industry: p53; Advertising Archives: p54; Hulton Archive: p60; Topham AP: p61 (bottom); The Wiener Library: p64; Institute of Contemporary History and Wiener Library limited/David Olere: p67, p72; Zofja Rozenstrauch; Rubin Mass Ltd., Jerusalem: p69; Bettman/Corbis: p79, p81; Corbis: p80; Ranan Lurie N.Y: p.82; Kevin Weaver/ Hulton Archive: p86, p89; Associated Press: p88; Popperfoto/Reuters: p91.

The publishers would also like to thank the following for permission to reproduce material in this book:
Simon & Schuster UK for extracts from The End of the American Century by Jeffery Robinson Copyright © Jeffery Robinson, 1997; University Press of the Pacific for extracts from Through the Russian Revolution by Albert Rhys Williams; Pen and Sword Books Ltd for extracts from Veterans by Richard van Emden and Steve Humphries; The Estate of Florence Farmborough c/o Constable & Robinson Ltd for extracts from A Nurse at the Russian Front 1914–18 by Florence Farmborough, 1974; Penguin for extracts from This Way for the Gas, Ladies and Gentlemen by Tadeusz Borowski © Penguin Book Ltd, 1967, and extracts from Total War by Peter Calvocoressi and Guy Wint, 1972, © Peter Calvocoressi and Guy Wint 1972; The Orion Publishing group for extracts from My American Century by Studs Terkel published by Pheonix Press and extracts from Keep Smiling Through the Home Front by Susan Briggs published by Weidenfeld & Nicolson; Oxford University Press for extracts from The Oxford Companion to the Second World War by A N Frankland; HarperCollins Publishers for extracts from A History of the Soviet Union by Geoffrey Hosking, © 1985 Geoffrey Hosking; Sheil Land Associates for extracts from Night by Elie Wiesel, published by Penguin Copyright © Les Editions de Minuit, 1958; The Random House Group for extracts from My War gone by, I miss it so by Anthony Loyd published by Doubleday. Used by permission of Transworld Publishers, a division of The Random House Group Limited.

Every effort has been made to trace and acknowledge ownership of copyright. The publishers will be glad to make suitable arrangements with any copyright holders whom it has not been possible to contact.

Artwork by Chris Rothero from Beehive Illustration and Richard Morris.

Orders: please contact Bookpoint Ltd, 130 Milton Park, Abingdon, Oxon OX14 4SB. Telephone: (44) 01235 827720. Fax: (44) 01235 400454. Lines are open from 9.00 - 6.00, Monday to Saturday, with a 24 hour message answering service. You can also order through our website www.hoddereducation.co.uk.

British Library Cataloguing in Publication Data
A catalogue record for this title is available from the British Library

ISBN-10: 0 340 86913 5
ISBN-13: 978 0 340 86913 0

First Published 2003
Impression number   10 9 8 7 6 5 4 3 2
Year   2007 2006 2005

Copyright © 2003 Neil DeMarco

Cover illustration from a painting by Coline U. Gill, 'Heavy Artillery' © Imperial War Museum
Layout by Cathy May (Endangered Species).
Colour Reproductions by Dot Gradations Ltd, UK.
Printed in Dubai for Hodder Murray, a division of Hodder Headline, 338 Euston Road, London NW1 3BH.

CONTENTS

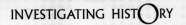
INTRODUCTION
The Twentieth Century – an Overview

History and the broken supermarket trolley

In 1900 people had good reason to look forward to the next one hundred years. They believed that the spread of factories (industrialisation) would mean a better standard of living for everyone – not just Europeans and Americans. The spread of **democracy** would mean that more people across the world would decide who would rule them. There would be social justice for workers, the poor and for women.

Unfortunately, history, like a broken supermarket trolley, seems to have a mind of its own and things rarely go in the direction people expect. By the early 1900s it was already clear that the major European powers were preparing for war. They were still continuing with the squabbles of the nineteenth century: they wanted more land and bigger **empires**, bigger navies and armies. Each nation became frightened by the power of the others and so they got together to form alliances. Britain joined up with France and Russia; Germany with Austria. These alliances made them feel more confident and aggressive.

SOURCE Ⓐ

CC the kitten, the world's first cloned domestic cat, with her 'mum', Allie, in 2002. When this book was written the cloning (or making identical copies) of humans was illegal – but for how much longer …?

Impact of World Wars

When, in June 1914, the heir to the throne of the Austrian Empire was assassinated by a Serb, Austria decided to take its revenge against Serbia and invaded. However, Serbia had an alliance with Russia, and Russia with France. Germany came to the aid of Austria. One by one, the powers of Europe were pulled into the war by their alliances.

The Great War of 1914–18 had a devastating effect on Europe. It not only led to the deaths of more than eight million people but it also changed people's ideas. Some were no longer willing to accept the idea that monarchs or parliaments were the best way to rule a country. They chose, instead, **Communism** or **Fascism**. Russia became Communist in 1917, Italy became Fascist in 1922 and Germany in 1933. These were depressing times for those who believed in democracy.

This hostility to democracy spread to the Far East where Japan imitated what Fascist Italy and Nazi Germany were doing. Japan also began bullying its weaker neighbours to gain more land and in 1941 took on the United States and Britain as part of its plan to control the whole of South East Asia. In this way, the war, which had begun in 1939 as a European war, now became the Second *World* War.

Fortunately, the Second World War led to the defeat of these three 'empires', but it was soon replaced by another 'war' – the **Cold War** – between the United States and the Communist Soviet Union, as Russia was now called. The end of the war also brought about the rapid collapse of the empires of the European powers, as the **colonies** of Britain and France achieved their freedom – though sometimes they had to fight for it.

THINK ABOUT IT

1. An optimist is someone who always looks on the bright side of a situation. Why were people in 1900 optimists?

2. Why were the decades after the Great War depressing ones for *democrats*?

3. What were the good and bad consequences of the Second World War?

4. Do you think people have much reason to be *optimistic* about the twenty-first century? Think about:
   - present-day conflicts and how they might end
   - developments in science and medicine – both good and bad
   - the chances of an end to hunger and poverty

The New Terror

Some of these new nations have been stable and successful but others have not. In some cases, religion has become the cause, once again, of conflict and tension. These conflicts go back a long way: Catholic against Protestant in Northern Ireland, Muslim against Hindu in India, and Muslim against Christian. This book finishes with the terrorist attacks on the United States on September 11, 2001. It is thought that these acts of terror were carried out by members of the terrorist group al-Qaeda (see page 90). The increase in world tension which has come about because of the attacks looks like dominating world politics for some time to come.

CHAPTER 1

War and Change

How did the First World War change British society?

In this chapter you will:

- Examine why men joined up and how the government encouraged them to enlist.
- Consider why some men's attitudes to the war changed.
- Imagine what it was like to fight in the war.
- Investigate how the war affected the position of women in Britain.

SOURCE A *British soldiers on their way to the front line for the first day of the Battle of the Somme. You can see wire-cutters on the ends of their rifles and the man at the front has a pair of heavy-duty cutters in his hands. Very few got far enough to be able to use their wire-cutters on the German barbed wire.*

The First World War, or the Great War as it was known then, broke out in August 1914 and British men were enthusiastic about it. (See the Introduction, page 5, for an explanation of its causes). In the first two months of the war 736,000 men volunteered. They were confident that the war would be over by Christmas, and most saw it as a great adventure and a chance to impress the girls with their smart uniforms.

THINK ABOUT IT

1. Some men joined up mainly because they were patriotic and wanted to defend their country from a dangerous enemy, Germany. Others joined up mostly for personal reasons, such as adventure or to do with their families. Do you think Robert Burns joined up mainly for patriotic or personal reasons?

2. Why do you think men who weren't in uniform were sometimes insulted in public and how would it have affected the men?

3. Do you think young people today are as patriotic as those in 1914? Explain your answer, giving reasons for your opinion.

4. Source B is an example of a recount text. Your task is to re-write the source as a formal report, which explains why men volunteered for the army in 1914. So:
   - You need to make it formal; it is an official report.
   - Avoid the use of the first person; use the third person instead.
   - Make sure each paragraph discusses at least one reason in turn and in detail.

SOURCE B

Robert Burns was 103 years old when he was interviewed, but he remembered very clearly why he volunteered for the British army in 1914:

'Everywhere you went in Glasgow, there were great big posters of Kitchener [the Minister for War in charge of recruiting men for the army] with his finger pointing at you, "Your King And Country Need You". No matter where you went, it seemed to be pointing at you personally.

I thought to myself, I want to do something like this, so I went to a recruiting office and the sergeant asked how old I was. I said that I was 18 and a bit and he said, "Oh you're too young, go back to your mother." A fortnight or so after that, I met a good pal who was trying to join up and I told him what had happened, and he told me to follow him and when we got to the recruiting office to tell a little fib. You had to be 19 to join up in those days, so it was a little fib because I was only a couple of months off being of age. I told my fib, was given a shilling, and I was in the army.

I think it was excitement more than anything that made me join up. I was too young to understand what **patriotism** really was. I lived in the country and there were not many boys my age, so I thought it would be nice to be with a lot of lads on something of a picnic, because we all thought the war would be over by Christmas. When I told the manager of the insurance company I wanted to join up, he said, "Well, it'll be a nice six-month holiday for you, yes, you join up." At 18 and 19 years of age, one is not very clever.

You stop, you look and you listen to other people and you think that if they are doing something, why can't I? My father had been in uniform practically from the day war was declared and I thought, I'll do what my father does. By the end of the war all the family was in uniform, my father, myself, a younger brother and two sisters, which only left my mother at home to run a hotel out in the country.'

Quoted in Veterans, *by Richard van Emden and Steve Humphries, 1998.*

How did the government persuade men to enlist?

When war broke out in August 1914, Britain was the only country which relied on volunteers for its armed forces. The government did not introduce **conscription** until January 1916. This meant that Britain's leaders had to encourage and persuade men to join up using various forms of **propaganda**.

The propaganda was very successful. The government appealed to their patriotism and sense of honour. It was their duty to defend their country and their families against the evil 'Huns' – the insulting term used for the Germans. Some of this propaganda told of the German murder of Belgian civilians. The Germans did execute Belgian civilians but the stories about them mutilating women and girls were made up.

A wounded British soldier pleads for water from a German nurse.

This British poster was cleverly designed to increase anti-German feeling and encourage men to enlist to stop more ill-treatment of British wounded. It also shows a very negative view of German women

SOURCE Ⓐ

The Red Cross helped the wounded on both sides.

The Iron Cross is a German medal awarded for great bravery.

This is a typically unflattering caricature of Germans.

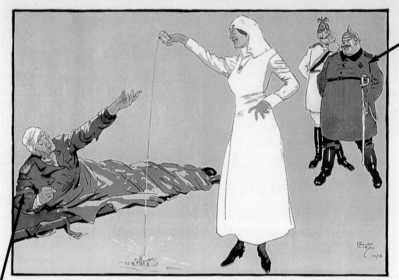

RED CROSS OR IRON CROSS?

WOUNDED AND A PRISONER OUR SOLDIER CRIES FOR WATER.

THE GERMAN "SISTER" POURS IT ON THE GROUND BEFORE HIS EYES.

THERE IS NO WOMAN IN BRITAIN WHO WOULD DO IT.

THERE IS NO WOMAN IN BRITAIN WHO WILL FORGET IT.

White Feather campaign

If men didn't join up out of a sense of duty, then the government also tried to shame men into enlisting. Would they allow *other* men to do their fighting for them? Would they sit at home while their fellow Britons were dying in the fields of France and Belgium to defend their families and country? There were other ways of shaming men into enlisting. Women would hand out white feathers – a symbol of cowardice – to any man fit for service and not in a military uniform. Public humiliation like this was more than most men could bear.

The government also agreed that those men who joined up together with their pals would be allowed to serve together. These units were called 'Pals Battalions'. (There were usually about 700 soldiers in a battalion.) Sometimes, local football and cricket teams would join together, or perhaps groups from the same village, or streets in a town. This was a very effective way of recruiting volunteers.

However, the government hadn't thought ahead. In 1916, during the Battle of the Somme, many thousands of these 'pals' were killed. The fact that they often came from the same small communities made the effect even more terrible.

Others simply joined up because the army paid more than their civilian jobs or because they were unemployed. Convicted criminals were sometimes given the choice of serving their sentence in prison or joining the army.

Conscientious Objectors

Not all men were willing to fight. Some, called conscientious objectors (COs), refused to fight because it was against their beliefs to kill or harm another human being. This is called **pacifism**. There were 16,500 COs and the government allowed them to do non-combatant duties in the army. This meant, for example, acting as stretcher-bearers in the medical corps, or as drivers, or clerical workers. In these jobs they would never have to kill anyone. Most accepted this offer but a small minority of 1,500 men, called absolutists, refused to do *any* activity related to the military. They were sent to prison. When the war ended, these men were kept in prison for an extra six months. This meant they had less chance of finding a job.

THINK ABOUT IT

Look at the British poster (Source A). Why was it such an effective poster? Comment on the following points:
- The contrast between Red Cross and Iron Cross
- The caricature of the two German officers
- The reaction of the German nurse (sister) to the plea by the British soldier
- The likely response of British men and women to seeing this poster

STOP AND REFLECT: Write a paragraph summing up ways in which men were encouraged to enlist.

Why did some soldiers' views about the war change?

The reality

It didn't take long for some men to realise that war was not a great adventure. The battles of 1915 and 1916 achieved little. The Battle of Loos, in which Robert Burns fought, lasted three weeks and cost 60,000 British casualties (killed and wounded). The Battle of the Somme in 1916 cost the lives of 20,000 Britons on its first day, July 1 – most of them in the first two hours. Many British soldiers were soon very angry about the way their generals planned and carried out this battle. It went on for five pointless months and claimed 400,000 British casualties. Though many of these men may have hated the war and couldn't see any point in it by now, they wouldn't run away. The believed that **desertion** was a coward's way out of the fighting and this wasn't honourable. Getting *deliberately* wounded (see Source A) so that you had to get sent back to Britain was also not honourable and you could be shot by the army.

A wound, as long as it wasn't too serious, was called a 'blighty' – Blighty was the soldier's slang for Britain – because it could get you sent home for treatment. But if a soldier stuck a leg or arm above the trench to get shot on purpose, fellow soldiers would think he was a coward. On the other hand, if he got a 'blighty' in a battle, then his comrades or fellow soldiers were pleased for him.

Soldiers in the trenches carried on fighting to earn the respect of other soldiers and to look out for each other. This is called comradeship and it was the most important reason to explain why they went on with the war.

After the war, some soldiers felt let down by the way the government failed to find them jobs or provide decent pensions for those disabled by the war. One soldier, interviewed in 1970, was still angry. 'I'd never fight for my country again', he said.

SOURCE Ⓐ

Robert Burns fought at the Battle of Loos in September 1915. His feelings about the war seemed to have changed by then:

'The strain took its toll at the Front, but you became hardened to it all. Oh yes, no doubt about it, you get hardened, and you wonder all the time when it's going to finish. You are hoping for a Blighty one, a wound that's not serious, in the arm or wrist, that would get you back home. I hoped to get a Blighty and I know those who looked for one, but getting one in the right place was difficult. At the Battle of Loos, the chappie sitting next to me was lying down with his legs in the air. I said "Keep your legs down."

"Why?"

I said,"You'll get shot."

He said, "I want to get shot in the leg. I want a Blighty one, then I won't have to go on any further. I don't want to stand up and get shot in the stomach."

Then another chap next to us said, "Good idea that" and he did the same.'

Quoted in **Veterans,** *by Richard van Emden and* **Steve Humphries, 1998.**

THINK ABOUT IT

1. What does Source B suggest about the morale of some British soldiers?

2. Do you think that soldiers who got themselves deliberately wounded to get out of the fighting were cowards?

3. Men who shot themselves or got themselves deliberately shot could face execution by the army command. Was the army right to do this?

4. Read Source A. With a partner identify the evidence that Burns, and other soldiers like him, had changed their views about the war from the views in Source B on page 7? You can also use Source B in your answer and, as you read, note down any key phrases you might refer to.

Set out your answer like this:

'It's clear from Source B on page 7 that Robert Burns and others like him were very keen to fight. The reasons he wanted to fight included …

However, by the time he fought at the Battle of Loos, his views seemed to have changed. For example …

This is supported by what some of his fellow soldiers did. One of them actually wanted …

In conclusion, men like Burns seemed to have had enough of the war. Most wanted an 'honourable' way out but some were so desperate to get out of the fighting that …'

SOURCE B

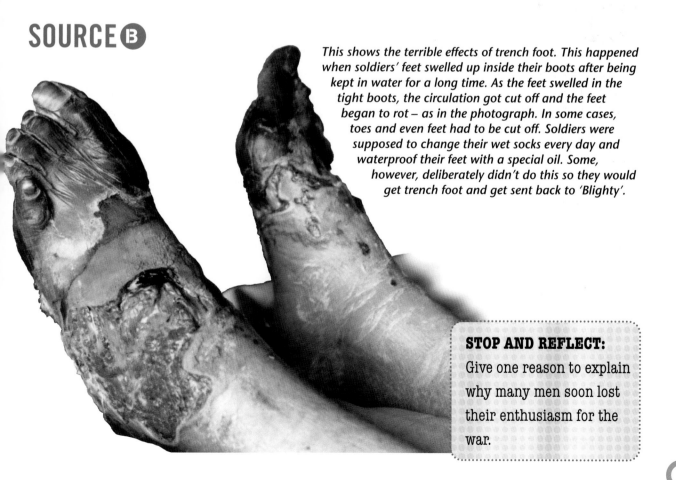

This shows the terrible effects of trench foot. This happened when soldiers' feet swelled up inside their boots after being kept in water for a long time. As the feet swelled in the tight boots, the circulation got cut off and the feet began to rot – as in the photograph. In some cases, toes and even feet had to be cut off. Soldiers were supposed to change their wet socks every day and waterproof their feet with a special oil. Some, however, deliberately didn't do this so they would get trench foot and get sent back to 'Blighty'.

STOP AND REFLECT:
Give one reason to explain why many men soon lost their enthusiasm for the war.

What was life like in the trenches?

Life in a First World War trench was mostly one of boredom and routine duties. Occasionally, there were brief periods of sheer terror when the enemy shelled your section of the front line or you were sent on a night-time raid into the German trenches to capture prisoners for questioning.

Sometimes both sides agreed truces – periods when there was no fighting. The Christmas truce of 1914 is the most famous and lasted for several days. The men also agreed truces during bad weather to repair their own trenches or to collect the wounded and dead from No Man's Land after a battle.

Soldiers didn't spend the whole war in the front line – perhaps eight days at one time. After that, you would be sent further back into a reserve or support trench where you were fairly safe (see the illustration of a trench system on page 14). After that, there was a spell away from the front altogether, in a village or town where you could wash and get 'deloused' (rid of the lice).

SOURCE Ⓐ

◄ January 1915 ◄

TRENCH NEWS
Beginner's Special

THE ARMY'S GOOD FOOD GUIDE

Do you like animals? Are you fond of dogs? Then trench sausages are just the thing for you! And if you have the runs, then our specially trained chefs have the cure ...

GET TO KNOW YOUR WAY AROUND THE TRENCH SYSTEM:

ADVERTISEMENT:

New stock of lice just in!

HOW TO SURVIVE – DO'S AND DON'T

HOW TO AVOID TRENCH FOOT:

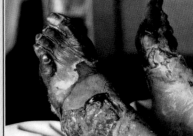

What happens to your feet if you get trench fo You have been warned!

HOW TO GET RID OF LICE:

LATRINES — What they are and w you should be careful when using them

A BLIGHTY — What it is and how not to get on

Troops produced their own newsletters for their regiments or battalions. They were often humorous and contained fake advertisements like the one in Source B.

Hygiene

Lice are small insects which feed off the blood of their victims. Their bites cause intense itching which leads to blisters, boils, and trench fever (similar to **typhus**). The eggs of lice were very difficult to get rid of. Body heat made the lice hatch out from the seams of clothes where they were laid. One way of killing them was to run the flame of a candle along the seam and listen to the 'pop' of the eggs as they exploded. The soldiers' slang for a louse was a 'chat', and the expression 'chatting' comes from this practice of groups of men getting together to kill off lice.

One part of trench life which soldiers hated was the lack of personal hygiene. Washing was very difficult and latrines (toilets) very primitive. Latrines were pits dug in side trenches, or saps, leading off from the main trenches. A long plank of wood with several holes cut into it was placed over the pit. When it was nearly full of waste it was filled in with earth and a new one dug. Soldiers didn't like using these latrines – and not just because of the terrible smell. The Germans knew where the latrines were and every now and then they would fire shells into them, just in case someone was using one at the time.

Humour played an important role in helping soldiers get through their time in the trenches. A favourite target for the men's jokes was army food. Sausages were known as 'barkers' because, it was believed, the meat in them came from dogs. Army cheese was called 'bung' because of the constipation it caused.

THINK ABOUT IT

Source A is the outline of what a newsletter might have looked like. Using Source A as a model, design your own newspaper. Copy this into your file or exercise book and fill in the stories suggested or you can make up your own. Re-read pages 10–11 first.

SOURCE B

BE IN THE FASHION.

Why have Cats, Dogs, Canaries, Rabbits, Parrots, etc.?

LICE!

EVERY CONCEIVABLE SHADE SUPPLIED:—BLUE BACKS, BLACK BACKS, RED BACKS, GREY BACKS, WHITE BACKS. ¶ ALSO IN A DELICATE PINK SHADE AND WITH VARIEGATED STRIPES. ¶ PURE THOROUGH-BREDS FROM OUR OWN SEAMS. ¶ MOST CLINGING, AFFECTIONATE, AND TAKING WAYS. ¶ VERY PROLIFIC, HARDY, AND WILL LIVE ANYWHERE. ¶ ONCE YOU HAVE THEM YOU WILL NEVER BE WITHOUT.

In Dainty Pochettes at 2/- per Thousand.

Write at once to E. R. M. CRACK,

Telegraphic Address: "Hitchy Koo." CHAT VILLA, CRUMBY.

An 'advertisement' in a soldiers' newsletter for lice.

STOP AND REFLECT: If the conditions in the trenches were so bad, why do you think the soldiers put up with them? Think about:
- What the army commanders might do to men who refused to fight in the trenches.
- What other soldiers might think about them.
- The importance of comradeship in keeping up morale.

What was it like to fight in the war?

'Going over the top'

Occasionally soldiers were ordered to leave their trenches, where they were reasonably safe, to attack the enemy trenches across 'no-man's-land'. The chances of an attack like this succeeding, in full view of the enemy, were slight. A machine gun could fire 8–10 bullets a second and the attackers had no protection against the hail of steel fired at them.

The worst part was waiting for the order to 'go over the top' of your own trench and advance through the paths cut in your own barbed wire towards the enemy's barbed wire and trenches (see Source A). However, once the officer blew his whistle for the attack, soldiers often commented that their fear left them as their training took over.

SOURCE Ⓐ

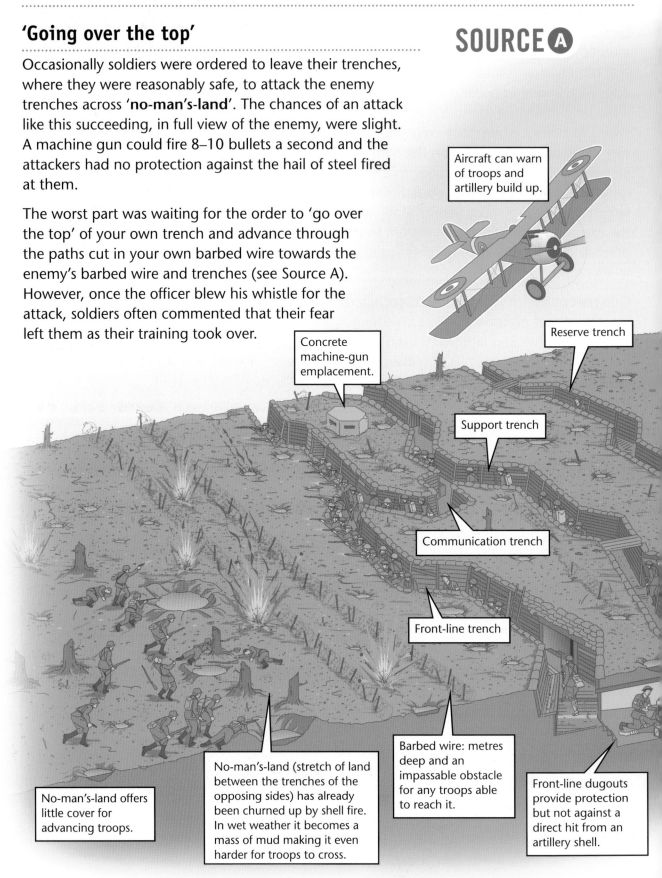

Aircraft can warn of troops and artillery build up.

Concrete machine-gun emplacement.

Reserve trench

Support trench

Communication trench

Front-line trench

No-man's-land offers little cover for advancing troops.

No-man's-land (stretch of land between the trenches of the opposing sides) has already been churned up by shell fire. In wet weather it becomes a mass of mud making it even harder for troops to cross.

Barbed wire: metres deep and an impassable obstacle for any troops able to reach it.

Front-line dugouts provide protection but not against a direct hit from an artillery shell.

SOURCE Ⓑ

Norman Collins was an officer in the Scottish 51st Highland Division. He was 19 when he took part in the Battle of the Somme in 1916. He died in 1998.

'You are very aware of the example you are setting the men; if they saw you funking it – showing fear – they wouldn't think much of you. They looked to me for encouragement, and you made jokes if you could … All the time I've no doubt whatsoever that I was as frightened as anything and hoping, a faint hope, that I would survive.

After any battle, you always had men lying out in no-man's-land, crying in agony and lying out there all night long in the dark, in the rain. You couldn't get them in and in any case they would never have survived. But you had a choice. They could die in agony or you could shoot them.

You were shown how to do the thing very cleanly. You put your .45 revolver muzzle against the back of his head and pulled the trigger and immediately the whole of the front skull came away and exposed the brain, just blown off. A lead bullet hit the inside of the skull, and they were dead instantly. There was no pain about it, but I can honestly say this, that I never had the courage – because that's what it took – I never had the courage myself to shoot a wounded soldier.

It's a tremendous thing to shoot a friend, even though he's in agony, and I just didn't have the courage to do it.'

Quoted in Veterans, *by Richard van Emden and Steve Humphries, 1998.*

Long-range artillery is placed about 5 km behind the front line. These guns fire at advancing enemy troops.

Communication trenches allow supplies and reserves to be brought forward without exposing them to enemy fire.

A deep dugout. German ones could be 15 metres below ground and well enough constructed to withstand shell fire.

The Trench System
This illustration shows how difficult it was to launch a successful attack on the enemy's trenches and why so many failed.

THINK ABOUT IT

1. Look at Source A. What does it tell you about why attacks failed so often? Think about:
   ● The advantages the defenders had.
   ● The disadvantages for those who were attacking.
2. Officers like Norman Collins, especially as young as he was, had to show many qualities and had many responsibilities. What evidence is there in Source B that officers like Collins had to:
   ● be mature
   ● set an example to others
   ● not show their own fear
   ● make terrible decisions?

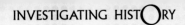

How far did the war affect the position of women? (1)

Today women – in law – have equal opportunities with men. They have the same career opportunities and should be paid the same as men for doing the same job. But it wasn't always like this.

Before the Great War, women didn't usually work. There were some jobs which they could do – but only if they weren't married. Working as secretaries, shop assistants and teachers for middle class women was acceptable but, once a woman married, she gave up her job to look after the home and her husband.

Many women were not happy with this. Some wanted to change the system and the laws, which, for example, stopped married women from working as doctors, solicitors, and teachers. But to change the law, you needed to have a voice in parliament and women didn't – they weren't allowed to become Members of Parliament or even vote in elections. Towards the end of the nineteenth century, women began campaigning for the suffrage – the right to vote. These women were known as suffragettes.

SOURCE Ⓐ

Lillian Christofas, born in 1896, came from a wealthy, upper-middle class family with several servants. Her father decided that she would marry a man called Edward, who was wealthy and educated. Lillian did not want to marry him and begged her mother to speak to her father.

'Well, she talked to my father but she might have talked to a brick wall. My father said I had to marry him, and I had to marry him. There was no argument about it ...

[My mother said to my father,] "You're making a very big mistake. That man is not for her."

My father turned round and said, "Will you please be quiet. You know nothing about these things." My mother was so humiliated, because he said all that in front of me. I think she wanted the earth to open and swallow her up ...

Edward came down for the weekend and asked if he might take me for a walk. This was the first time I had been out alone with him, and we went for a country walk. We went over a field and there was a little stile we had to cross, and I wouldn't do it until he turned

around and put his back on me. I was so shy. I was afraid I might show my ankle or a little bit of my petticoat.

We had the wedding, and I was so ill with nerves I don't know how I wasn't sick during the reception. I couldn't travel, I was so ill. So we stayed at the Metropole and had separate rooms, thank God! So that was my first night of marriage in 1915.

The next day we travelled to London and my troubles started. I went in to it like a lamb to the slaughterhouse. I hadn't the faintest idea what an adult man had down there. He was very highly sexed and I didn't know anything about sex ... I was in a state of terror, in a state of physical agony, and I went through the tortures of hell.'

The marriage was not a success but ended with Edward's death in the Great War. As Lillian put it, 'He died and I was free'. Her father found her another husband but this time Lillian refused to marry him. Instead, she married his Greek friend, despite her father's strong opposition. The marriage also ended with his death – but after over fifty happy years.

From The Nineties: Personal Recollections of the 20th Century, *edited by G. Wood and P Thompson, 1993.*

SOURCE B

Not many men supported the suffragettes and there was a lot of anti-suffragette material published, such as this 1909 postcard. The media treated feminists in the 1970s in a similar way.

THINK ABOUT IT

1. Lillian uses a metaphor and a simile in her account:
   a) 'she wanted the earth to open and swallow her up', and
   b) 'like a lamb to the slaughterhouse'.

   How does Lillian's choice of imagery tell you how she felt?

2. What does Lillian's account tell us about the relationship before 1914 between:
   a) daughters and fathers
   b) husbands and wives?

3. How can we tell from the source that Lillian had led a very sheltered life and was not prepared for married life?

4. What do you think Lillian meant by 'He died and I was free'?

5. In what ways have the lives of young women today changed from the life Lillian had?

STOP AND REFLECT:

Why did the Suffragettes face a difficult task in achieving their aims? Think about: the hostility of men; the attitudes of other women; the holders of political power in the country.

How far did the war affect the position of women? (2)

SOURCE A

A French magazine illustration from 1917 showing British army women as carpenters.

There were limits to what women wanted to achieve. Even the suffragettes felt they had to show that women who wanted the vote could make good housewives as well. In the photograph on the right Mrs Martyn, a suffragette, shows that she makes jam at home.

Women and the Great War

The war opened up many new opportunities for women. From 1917, they began serving in the armed forces for the first time. Women could join Women's Army Auxiliary Corps, the Women's Royal Naval Service and the Women's Royal Air Force. In all, about 100,000 served in these organisations. Some got close to the front line as nurses and as nursing assistants in the Volunteer Aid Detachments. One British nurse, Edith Cavell, was shot by the Germans for helping British soldiers escape back to their own side.

There were also big changes on the home front. The Suffragettes stopped their campaign for the vote while the war was on and campaigned, instead, for a woman's Right To Serve. In 1915, 60,000 women marched to demand a role for women in the war. At first, the government didn't want women to get involved in the war effort and told them to stay at home. However, as the casualties from the war increased, the government changed its mind. Suddenly it was very keen for women to take over the jobs of the men serving in the armed forces.

The number of women in the munitions industry, making weapons and shells, increased from 200,000 in 1914 to 900,000 in 1918. This dangerous work damaged women's health – the chemicals turned their skin yellow, gave some cancer and made them sterile. Others found work in shipyards, drove trams, buses, and ambulances. Some became policewomen. These were new experiences for women – only one thing didn't change. They still got paid much less than the men who had done these jobs before the war.

SOURCE B

After the war

In December 1918 women aged 30 or over were given the right to vote – though men were now able to vote at the age of 21. It wasn't until 1928 that women were finally able to vote on the same terms as men – at the age of 21. In 1919 single women who married could carry on working as doctors, solicitors, and civil servants, instead of having to give up their jobs. But even as late as 1951 women made up only 8% of these professions – up by just 2% from the 1911 figure. Married women teachers would have to wait until 1944 before they were allowed to keep their jobs.

THINK ABOUT IT

Write a description of the situation for women before the war and then show what changes there were during and after the war. How important were the changes?

STOP AND REFLECT: Why was the First World War a step forward in getting votes for women? Explain in one sentence.

Pulling it Together

How did the First World War change British society?

The six points below should each take up a paragraph in a piece of analysis.

- Introduction: why British men and women in 1914 were so enthusiastic. Explain the role of: patriotism, adventure, peer group pressure.
- Why some opposed the war from the start. Include religious beliefs, pacifism.
- Why some soldiers changed their attitude during the war. Use connectives relating to time. Include trench conditions, casualties, lack of success.

- Why most soldiers continued to fight on. Include patriotism and comradeship.
- How far the role of women changed as a result of the war. Include contrasting connectives. Include conditions before 1914, what they did during it and changes after it.
- Finish with a conclusion, such as: 'The war affected the British people in different ways. Some remained very patriotic while others … Life for women improved because … but in some ways it didn't change very much …'

CHAPTER 2
The Nazi Dictatorship
Why was Hitler so popular in Germany?

In this chapter you will:

- Examine why Hitler was so popular with the German people.
- Find out how he persuaded Germans to support him.
- Investigate who benefited and who suffered from Nazi rule.
- Examine why Hitler got his way in Europe.

'The stab in the back'?

After the failure of Germany's last military offensive of the First World War in March, 1918, the German army was gradually driven back by the Allied armies of Britain, France and the United States. One by one, Germany's allies surrendered until the Germans were left on their own against the Allies and agreed to an **armistice** on November 11, 1918.

The German army had retreated slowly, without panicking and many of its soldiers didn't feel like a defeated army. Some were willing to go on fighting and blamed the new democratic government for 'stabbing the army in the back', for betraying the soldiers by agreeing to surrender. Adolf Hitler, who later became **dictator** of Germany, constantly repeated the idea of this 'stab in the back'. He called these democratic politicians who signed the armistice 'the November criminals'.

SOURCE Ⓐ

This is the view of an experienced front-line British army chaplain or priest, writing about the Germans on November 7, 1918 – just four days before the war ended.

'The Germans are fighting a clever defensive campaign … and have plenty of time to get back and form new machine-gun posts, which cause us heavy casualties as we advance … We all, except perhaps the senior officers who don't see anything of the fighting or the morale of the Germans, expect another six months' of fighting.'

Quoted in The Pity of War, *Niall Ferguson, 1998.*

THINK ABOUT IT

1. What was the 'stab in the back' theory?

2. Describe why the Treaty of Versailles caused so much anger among Germans like Hitler.

SOURCE Ⓑ

Map of Germany after the Treaty of Versailles.

How did the Treaty of Versailles help the Nazis?

Hitler became even more popular in Germany when he criticised the Treaty of Versailles. This was the treaty drawn up by the British, French, and Americans which Germany had to sign. The new government which took over from the Kaiser (Emperor of Germany) was forced to take the blame for the defeat and the Treaty of Versailles which followed.

The treaty, from Germany's point of view, was harsh. The Germans had to hand over territory to France and Poland and nearly £7 billion to Britain and France to pay reparations or compensation for the damage caused in the war. The German army was cut to just 100,000 men and there were to be no air force, submarines or tanks at all.

As a result of the treaty, Germany lost 13% of its land and millions of German-speaking people were forced to become citizens of other countries, such as Czechoslovakia and Poland.

Hitler found it easy to get people to listen to his criticisms of the treaty. He said it was harsh and humiliated the German people. If he ever became leader of Germany, he said, he would tear the treaty to pieces.

Was the Treaty too harsh?

Some historians have criticised the treaty for punishing Germans so harshly that eventually they turned against their new government and democracy and chose Hitler instead. Some British economists at the time argued that Germany wouldn't be able to afford to pay the costs of the war because it had to hand over so many of its coal and iron-producing areas to other countries.

However, the Germans didn't have that much reason to complain. At the end of 1917, Russia had surrendered to Germany. The treaty that Germany forced Russia to sign in March 1918 was much worse than the Treaty of Versailles. Germany lost about 10% of its population but Russia lost 25%!

The Rhineland. This area was demilitarised so that no German troops could stay there.

This area, called the Polish Corridor, was taken from Germany and given to Poland. This meant that East Prussia was now cut off from the rest of Germany.

Alsace-Lorraine: returned to France.

Austria. Seven million Germans lived here. They were not allowed to unite with Germany.

This was the Sudetenland. Three million Germans lived there and they became citizens of Czechoslovakia.

How did Hitler persuade Germans to support him?

Economic problems: savings and jobs

The new, democratic government of Germany started its life in the town of Weimar, near Berlin. So, Germany, between 1919 and 1933, is known as Weimar Germany. In 1923 the economy collapsed as **hyper-inflation** wiped out the savings of millions of Germans. Many of these were middle class people – small businessmen and professionals, such as doctors and lawyers. They never forgave the government for allowing this to happen.

The worst problem was the Great Depression of 1929–33. A **depression** is an economic crisis in which many firms go out of business and workers lose their jobs. In 1932, 6 million people were out of work in Germany – about 25% of the working population. The government couldn't solve the crisis or find a way to put these people back to work.

Some turned to Germany's **Communists**, who promised the same policies as Lenin in Russia (see Chapter 3). This deeply worried rich businessmen who feared that the Communists would take their property and wealth from them. So, for the first time, many millions began to listen to Hitler and his National Socialist (Nazi) Party.

SOURCE Ⓐ

Toys were hard to come by in Germany in 1923 so these children have to make do with bundles of German banknotes worth tens of millions of marks. This makes clear how worthless the currency became in the hyper-inflation of 1923.

Hitler's attack on democracy

Hitler was a very powerful speaker. His speeches had only a few ideas in them but he kept repeating those ideas. In 1932 a typical Hitler speech would have made the following points:

- The German people and army were betrayed by the democratic politicians in 1918 who begged for peace when the army could have continued to fight.

- These politicians allowed Germany to be humiliated by the Treaty of Versailles.

- The Weimar government ruined people's lives in the crisis of 1923.

- The same government is ruining the lives of many millions more in the present economic crisis which started in 1929.

- Communists are close to seizing power and only the Nazis can stop them.

THINK ABOUT IT

Your task is to write a speech for Hitler in November 1932, just a few days before the election and two months before Hitler became Chancellor or Prime Minister of Germany in January 1933. The five basic points to cover are shown on the left, starting with how Germany was betrayed by the democratic politicians who agreed to surrender in 1918.

Source A on page 20, and Source A opposite, are there to provide specific evidence for you to use in the speech. For example, Source A on page 20 clearly supports Hitler's view that the German army had plenty of fight left in it at the end of the war so you can use this in your speech, like this:

'We in the National Socialist Party have always believed that our glorious army was never defeated in 1918. It was betrayed by the cowardly politicians who begged for peace. Even at the very end of the war a British chaplain wrote admiringly of how our soldiers were "fighting a clever defensive campaign". Does this sound like a beaten army? No!

These same cowardly politicians then went on to agree to the humiliating terms of the Treaty of Versailles … (Use Source A on page 20 here)

Worse was to come in 1923 when hyper-inflation wiped out our people's savings. (Use Source B on page)

Now we find ourselves in a new economic crisis and Communists threatening to seize power…'

(Now finish Hitler's speech with a dramatic call on Germans to vote Nazi as the only way to save the nation from disaster.)

STOP AND REFLECT: How did Germany's economic problems help Hitler? Sum it up in two sentences:
- How the crisis of 1923 helped him.
- How the Great Depression helped him.

Who benefited from Hitler's rule?

SOURCE A

A German farmer's wife, Luise Essig, remembers a Nazi Harvest Festival:

'Thousands of farmers and young people from all over Germany travelled in special trains and then marched for hours to get as close to the front as possible. We all felt the same, the same happiness and joy. The Harvest Festival was the 'thank you' for the fact that we farmers had a future again. Things were looking up. I believe no statesman has ever been as loved as Adolf Hitler was then. It's all come flooding back to me. Those were happy times.'

SOURCE B

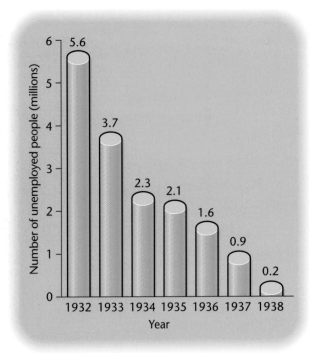

Unemployment levels in Germany, 1932–8.

Millions voted Nazi

It is worth remembering that Hitler came to power legally. He became Chancellor (or Prime Minister) in January 1933 because President Hindenburg asked him to take the post. He gave him the job because the Nazis had more votes than any other political party in Germany – though 37% of the vote (nearly 14 million votes) was the most they ever got before 1933. Even in the election of 1933, the Nazis didn't get a majority of the votes. Nonetheless, they were still very popular and the reason for this is that the Nazi Party had a very wide appeal to many different Germans.

Farmers were an important group who supported Hitler, as were middle class people, such as office workers and small business owners. People who lived in small towns and the country also found Hitler's views attractive. People who usually never bothered to vote found something in him which made them vote for the Nazis. Unemployed workers, though, preferred to vote for the Socialists or the Communists. However, Hitler's economic policies created millions of jobs and soon unemployed workers had reasons to be grateful to him.

Hitler spent billions of marks on boosting Germany's armed forces. In 1933 the government spent just 3 billion marks on the armed forces. By 1938 this had grown to 17 billion marks – nearly six times more. This meant many more jobs for miners, steel and iron workers. As a result, unemployment fell rapidly (see Source B).

SOURCE ©

Cheering crowds salute Hitler at a Nazi Party rally in 1938, in Nuremberg. Hitler gave himself the title 'Führer', or Leader, and the enthusiasm of these Germans for their Führer is obvious.

Propaganda

The Nazis also found ways of filling workers' leisure time. The Strength through Joy movement organised theatre trips and even free holidays on cruise ships. Though very few people actually got one of these trips, it didn't stop the Nazis from claiming that they looked after the workers.

The Berlin Olympics was a great propaganda victory for the Nazis since Germany won more gold medals than any other country – 33 gold medals to 24 by the USA. This, Hitler claimed, showed the superiority of the German race over 'inferior' races like black people and Jews.

THINK ABOUT IT

1. The man in charge of Nazi propaganda was Josef Goebbels. Goebbels was a very skilful Minister of Propaganda who used film and posters particularly well to get across the Nazi message. Your task here is make a short propaganda film in 1938 for Goebbels showing the Führer in the most favourable way. The chart opposite provides the instructions for the film director and editor, based on Sources A–D. A few examples have been filled in and your task is to complete the others.

SOURCE D

The start of the 100 m sprint from the Berlin Olympics. The black American athlete, Jesse Owens, on the right here, won the gold medal, as well as gold medals in the Long Jump, 200 m and relay. This did not please Hitler and he refused to present the medals to the winning athletes.

Source	Instructions to the editor and director on how to use the source	Commentary to go with the source
Source A	Interview Luise Essig. Ask her why she loves the Führer. Make it clear she is the wife of a farmer – the Führer doesn't like women working.	
Source B		'Millions have found work since we took over. In 1932, 6 million Germans were without work. Now…'
Source C		
Source D	We can't use all of this photo because …	

Women and girls

Women were encouraged to stay at home and raise children for Germany. Each married couple received a loan of 600 marks (equal to about four months' salary). The government allowed the couple to keep 150 marks of the loan as a gift for each child they had. After four children, they owed nothing. Mothers of eight children were given a gold medal on August 12 each year – the birthday of Hitler's mother. Pregnant women were discouraged from slimming and smoking – the Nazis believed both of these harmed the baby. The Nazis also disapproved of women perming their hair and wearing trousers or make-up.

Girls were taught different subjects from boys in school. The emphasis was on skills which they would find useful as wives and mothers. Cookery, health and fitness were especially important – fit girls would be able to have more babies. Not all young girls were happy about this. The school leaving certificate for Domestic Science was nick-named the 'Pudding Level'.

THINK ABOUT IT

2. In a group consider: if we in Britain elected someone into power with views similar to Hitler's, would people in other countries have the right to try and stop him becoming leader? Set out the case for and against other countries having this right

STOP AND REFLECT: Why were so many Germans enthusiastic supporters of Hitler? Write five sentences to sum up:
- Hitler's appeal to different social groups.
- The likely attitude of those who found work after Hitler came to power.
- The response of those in the armed forces to his policies.
- The effect of propaganda.
- How Germans would have felt after the Berlin Olympics.

SOURCE Ⓐ

Maths
Question 95:

'It costs 6 million RM (Reichmarks) to build a lunatic asylum. How many houses at 15,000 RM each could have been built for that amount?'

Question 97:

To keep a mentally ill person costs about 4 RM per day, a cripple 5.50 RM, a criminal 3.50 RM. Many civil servants [people who work for the government] get paid only 4 RM a day.

(a) Draw a diagram for these figures. There are about 300,000 mentally ill, epileptics etc. in care.

(b) How much do these people cost to keep in total, at a cost of 4 RM per head?'

Questions from a Maths textbook used in German schools during the Nazi period.

Everything in Hitler's Germany was used to get across the Nazi message – even Maths lessons, as you can see in Source A. Whether German pupils learned much Maths in these lessons was not as important as whether they learned to hate the same things and people as the Nazis. In Hitler's Germany it was important to hate.

Jews were supposed to be behind Communism. Here Russia is shown with the symbols of Communism – a hammer and sickle – on it. Was Germany next?

The features shown here are supposed to be typically Jewish: coarse, thick lips, big nose and straggly beard.

'Greedy' Jews were also supposed to become rich by lending money and charging huge rates of interest.

SOURCE Ⓑ

This is a typical example of Nazi propaganda against the Jews. One of the dafter Nazi ideas about the Jews was that they were supposed to be both businessmen and Communists – who are against privately-owned businesses. This picture was entitled 'The Eternal Jew'.

Jews were supposed to be cruel businessmen who worked their employees like slavedrivers.

Hitler's hate list

The list of people Hitler and the Nazis hated is a long one. Most of this hatred was to do with race. The Germans were a superior race, according to Hitler, and so they had the right to dominate 'inferior' races, such as Jews, but also gypsies, Slavs (such as Poles and Russians), and black people. Germans who were mentally ill and disabled were also targets because they 'damaged' the racial quality of the people.

Hitler added to this list people whose views he didn't like. Communists, Socialists, Christian priests, homosexuals, and **pacifists** were against Nazism and often ended up in prison.

It is important to remember that the policy of mass-murder of the Jews (the Holocaust) didn't start until 1941 – after the Second World War had begun. Before then, Jews in Germany were treated badly, persecuted and publicly humiliated, but it wasn't Nazi policy to kill them.

It is also true that **anti-Semitism** had existed in Europe for many centuries. Christians blamed Jews for the death of Christ, and in Medieval times they believed that Jews kidnapped and sacrificed Christian children as part of their religion. This prejudice made Hitler's task that much easier.

Boycott

On April 1, 1933, the Nazis called on Germans to **boycott** Jewish businesses and professionals, such as dentists and doctors. The boycott, though, only lasted one day. Jews were also banned from working for the government or as doctors, dentists and lawyers.

Some Jews – with the Nazi government's approval – decided to leave Germany. During 1933 and 1934, 60,000 out of Germany's 500,000 Jews left Germany for good. It wasn't easy, however, to find countries willing to let them in. Nonetheless, by the time Hitler stopped Jews from leaving Germany in 1941, 75% had left the country – though they first had to hand over their homes and businesses to the government at very low prices. One hundred thousand emigrated to the United States and 50,000 came to Britain.

The Nuremberg Laws

Many fanatical Nazis were unhappy with the slow progress of the measures against the Jews. They wanted harsher policies. In 1935 Hitler decided to give them what they wanted. The Nuremberg Laws:

- Banned marriages and sexual relations between Jews and non-Jews.

- Stopped Jews from being German citizens.

- Stopped Jews from using public facilities such as swimming pools and restaurants.

Most Germans didn't appear to be very concerned about what was happening to the Jews. In fact, many Germans seemed to welcome these laws. Most Jews simply hoped that things wouldn't get any worse and 'kept their heads down.' But they did get worse. In 1938 the Nazis began a policy of confiscating Jewish businesses. These were then sold off cheaply to Germans – a clever way of making them play a part in the Nazis' campaign. The aim of this policy was to encourage Jews to get out of Germany.

The Night of Broken Glass

On November 7, 1938, a 17-year-old Polish Jew shot dead a German diplomat in Paris in protest against the German government's anti-Semitism. The Nazi leaders quickly organised a wave of anti-Jewish attacks in which over 8,000 Jewish businesses and 200 synagogues were destroyed.

Surprisingly, the Nazi secret police, the Gestapo, took a dim view of any Nazis who stole from the Jews for their own benefit, as Source E makes clear. Over 30,000 Jewish men were arrested and sent to labour camps. Most of these were released within a couple of months but not before about a thousand had been murdered.

Mass killing begins

One policy which the Nazis tried to keep secret was the killing of Germans who were disabled or mentally ill. The Nazis had already begun a policy of sterilising such people so that they couldn't have children, but now this went a step further. Between the autumn of 1939 and August 1941, 70,000 disabled men, women, and children were killed for this reason.

Hitler was determined to make the German people a 'master race' (*Herrenvolk*). This master race would have no physical and mental weaknesses. There would, therefore, be no place for the disabled. Many of the victims were gassed with carbon monoxide. The government tried to keep the programme secret but details soon leaked out. A protest by a leading German Catholic bishop in August 1941 forced Hitler temporarily to stop the policy. It was soon re-started, but in greater secrecy.

SOURCE ⓒ

Ilustration of the Nazi campaign against the Jews, 1933–9

Why didn't the Germans oppose Hitler?

If Hitler was such a cruel leader, why was he so popular? The reason is that the vast majority of Germans did well out of Hitler's rule between 1933 and 1939. There were only about 500,000 Jews in Germany – less than 1% of the population. The other victims of Hitler's policies were also a small minority and most people didn't really care if they were badly treated. The few who did speak out against the Nazis were arrested and imprisoned. It was safer to ignore it all and enjoy the good times which Germany was now experiencing.

Some Germans alive today, like the woman quoted here who lived through the Nazi period, still have good memories: 'I thought it was a good time. I liked it … there was order and discipline. I thought it was a better time then.' For most Germans, that seemed enough.

SOURCE E

In December 1938, a Jewish family complained to the local police that a drunken member of a Nazi organisation called the SA, along with two others, had stolen some of their personal possessions from their home.

'After a few hours the Gestapo appeared. We told them what had happened and gave them the number on the uniform collar of the SA man that I had noticed. It was in May 1939 that my father sent a newspaper clipping to me in London with a report on the case. They were sentenced to long jail sentences. Unofficial crimes were forbidden in Nazi Germany.'

SOURCE D

A farming family, by Adolf Wissel. What the ideal German family should look like – according to the Nazis.

THINK ABOUT IT

1. Write a caption describing each of the events shown in Source C.

2. What attitude to disabled people is Source A (page 28) trying to encourage?

3. a) Why is the story in Source E so surprising?

   b) Why do you think the men who stole from the Jews in Source E were punished?

4. Why is the family in Source D the ideal family according to the Nazis?

5. Can you think of any groups of people in Britain today which some people don't care about? Why is that?

STOP AND REFLECT: Why was Hitler able to get away with his campaign against the Jews in Germany?
Give at least two reasons and explain why each worked to assist Hitler.

Why did Hitler get his way in Europe?

SOURCE A

A 14-year-old Austrian girl remembers the day she shook Hitler's hand:

'He came. Everything got quiet and we were so excited. I felt my heart up here in the throat. When he came to me I nearly forgot to give him my hand; I just looked at him and I saw good eyes. In my heart I promised him, "I will always be faithful to you because you are a good man" and I kept my promise.'

So far we have looked at what Hitler did inside Germany – his domestic policies. These pages investigate his foreign policy – the policies concerning other countries. His successes here are an important reason for his popularity in Germany in the 1930s, as you can see from Source A.

SOURCE B

Daladier, the Prime Minister of France.

David Low was a British cartoonist who strongly opposed Britain's policy of giving in to Hitler. Here he pokes fun at the leaders Britain, France and Italy and suggests that the vote in Austria wasn't really fair.

British Foreign Minister.   Neville Chamberlain.   Mussolini.

Hitler's attack on the Treaty of Versailles

Hitler, like many Germans, believed that the Treaty of Versailles had humiliated Germany (see page 21). Getting rid of the treaty was his first policy. In 1935 he announced that the German army would be increased from 100,000 men to 500,000. This was five times the limit set down by the treaty. Both Britain and France protested that this was against the treaty but did nothing. In fact, the British government then went on to agree that Germany should have a bigger navy. Hitler described the day that agreement was signed as 'the happiest of my life' but things were to get even better for him.

Hitler became more confident. In March 1936 he sent just 3,000 German troops into the Rhineland – an area which was not allowed to have soldiers in it, according to the Treaty of Versailles (see Source B, page 20–1). Hitler gambled that neither Britain nor France had the stomach for a war over the Rhineland and he was right. Hitler had issued secret orders to the troops to retreat if there was any military opposition from France, but the French wouldn't act without British support and Britain looked the other way.

Austria united with Germany

In 1937 Britain had a new prime minister, Neville Chamberlain. He supported the same policy towards Hitler as the previous prime minister, that is, he didn't want a confrontation with Germany. When Germany took over Austria in March 1938, the leaders of Britain, France, and Italy all accepted another increase in Germany's power without protest (see Source B). The next month, Hitler organised a plebiscite (vote) in Austria. According to the result, 99% of Austrians agreed that Austria and Germany should become one country.

Low hated Hitler. Why, then, has he drawn him like this?

What's missing from the pile of votes here?

Why is there only one box for 'Yes' (Ja) votes here?

Josef Goebbels, in charge of Hitler's propaganda.

Czechoslovakia disappears

Hitler had always claimed that German-speaking people should be part of the new Germany he was creating. Seven million Austrians were now part of this Greater Germany, but there were another 3 million Germans in a part of Czechoslovakia called the Sudetenland.

However, the Czechs were ready to fight to keep the Sudetenland. The Czech army was big and well-equipped. With the support of Britain and France, they could easily defeat Germany – as long as they got that support. Unfortunately for the Czechs, Neville Chamberlain, the British Prime Minister, and Daladier, the French leader, were no more willing to go to war to defend Czechoslovakia than they were to protect Austria.

Chamberlain, Daladier, Hitler and Mussolini, the dictator of Italy, all met at a conference in Munich in September 1938 to decide what to do. The Czech leader wasn't invited. Hitler promised that this was the last demand he would make. Germany would be complete with the Sudetenland, he promised. Chamberlain believed him and the four nations at Munich agreed that Hitler could take over the Sudetenland.

There was no stopping Hitler now. Six months later, in March 1939, German troops occupied the rest of Czechoslovakia. There were no Germans there. It was obvious that Hitler simply wanted to make Germany a bigger country, a Greater Germany. There were Germans in Poland, though. About a million Germans lived in the Polish Corridor (see Source B, page 21) and this obviously was Hitler's next target. At last Britain and France realised that Hitler could not be trusted, and they quickly promised to defend Poland if Germany attacked.

SOURCE C

'He drove from Heston airport to Buckingham Palace, where the crowd called for him, and within five minutes of his arrival he was standing on the balcony of the Palace with the King and Queen and Mrs Chamberlain.

The cries were all for "Neville" and he stood there waving his hand and smiling. For three minutes this demonstration lasted. Another welcome awaited the Prime Minister in Downing Street. Everywhere there were people cheering. One of the women there could find only these words to express her feelings, "The man who gave me back my son."'

The Guardian *newspaper report on Neville Chamberlain's return from the Munich Conference, October 1, 1938.*

SOURCE D

Nazi–Soviet Pact

Hitler didn't pay too much attention to this promise. He was convinced that Britain and France would do nothing to defend Poland. The only people he was really worried about were the Communists of the Soviet Union. If they signed an alliance with Britain, Germany could face a war on two fronts – against Britain and France in the West and against the Soviet Union in the East. So Hitler decided that he would sign an alliance or pact with the Soviet Union in August 1939. The Nazi–Soviet Pact astonished the world but the really shocking part of the pact was kept secret. Germany and the Soviet Union agreed to invade Poland and divide the country between them.

On September 1, 1939, German troops invaded Poland. Britain and France, to Hitler's surprise, declared war on Germany two days later. The Second World War had begun.

THINK ABOUT IT

1. What do Sources C and D suggest about the attitude of the British people to possibility of war with Germany over the Sudetenland in 1938?

2. What do you think the woman in Source C meant when she said, 'The man who gave me back my son'? (Clue: think about what would have happened if there had been a war between Britain and Germany then).

3. How useful are these sources in explaining the reasons for Chamberlain's policy towards Hitler?

4. 'Neville Chamberlain alone was to blame for the war with Germany because he didn't stand up to Hitler soon enough.' Using the sources and the text, explain whether you agree or disagree with this interpretation. You could include the following points in your answer:
   - British government policies before Chamberlain became Prime Minister
   - the role of the French government
   - the attitude of the British people.

Remember to provide evidence from more than one point of view so that your account is balanced. But, finish with a conclusion which shows what your view is.

A delighted Chamberlain leans from a window at 10 Downing Street to wave to a cheering crowd outside. This was on October 1, after his return from Munich.

STOP AND REFLECT: Why did Hitler's foreign policies make him even more popular in Germany? Write a paragraph summing up the main points from what you have learned.

Pulling it Together

Why was Hitler so popular in Germany?

This chapter started with the question 'Why was Hitler so popular in Germany?'. You should be ready by now to write a short essay in answer to this question, using the evidence which you have read in the chapter.

This is a formal piece of writing and you will need to structure your answer with an introduction, the main body of the essay, and a conclusion.

The first task is to find the evidence which you will use to back up your points. Copy this chart into your exercise book or file.

Hitler was popular because:	Evidence to support this:
1. He opposed the Treaty of Versailles	Read pages 20–1. Make notes about how terms of the treaty angered Germans: • land • reparations • military
2. The Weimar government failed to solve the unemployment crisis	Read page 22. Make notes about: • unemployment • fear of communism among wealthy Germans
3. His policies appealed to most of the German people	Read pages 22–3. Make notes about how Hitler appealed to Germans with his policies on: • jobs • Communists
4. He made Germany a great power again	Read pages 32–5. Make notes about: • rebuilding Germany's armed forces • Berlin Olympics • foreign policy successes

Now that you have collected the evidence, it is time to write the essay. Here is a writing frame which includes paragraph starters to help you set out the essay.

Planning frame	Writing frame – paragraph starters
Introduction	There is no doubt that Hitler was very popular among Germans in the 1930s for many different reasons.
Introduction to first paragraph Introduce the theme. ● Supporting evidence	His opposition to the Treaty of Versailles was popular because most Germans … This is supported by the terms of the treaty concerning …
Introduction to second paragraph Use a logical explanatory connective like 'In addition …' ● Supporting evidence ● Supporting evidence	In addition, Hitler's popularity was increased by the failure of the government … Between 1929 and 1932 unemployment … This was made worse by fears that …
Introduction to third paragraph Start with another logical connective which develops the argument. ● Supporting evidence ● Supporting evidence	Furthermore, when Hitler was in power from 1933 onwards his popularity increased because … A key point in support of this was his success in dealing with unemployment … He added to his popularity among rich Germans by …
Introduction to fourth paragraph Begin to draw towards an assessment. ● Supporting evidence ● Supporting evidence ● Supporting evidence	Perhaps his greatest success in the eyes of the people was … He increased Germany's armed forces … This new feeling of pride was added to in 1936 with … Finally, he reached the peak of his popularity in 1938 with …
Conclusion Make it clear that you are bringing the evidence together. Make a final decision based on the evidence.	Though Hitler was not popular with a minority of Germans, the evidence presented makes clear that … The most important reason for his success was …

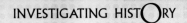

CHAPTER 3

Revolution!

Did the Russian Revolution really make life better for ordinary Russians?

In this chapter you will:

- **Decide why the Russians turned against the Tsar and overthrew him.**
- **Examine why the Russians had another revolution.**
- **Learn why there was a Russian Civil War.**
- **Investigate how Stalin changed the Soviet Union.**
- **Consider whether life for the people improved after the Communist revolution.**

SOURCE A

A British nurse describes the Russian front:

'A young artillery officer came to seek advice from our medical staff. He was depressed by the recent defeat and criticised the High Command. "They do not realise how exhausted our men are," he cried. "In their comfortable armchairs in their hotels far from the fighting, with the war-maps stretched before them, they put their finger on a town – 'Ah', they say, 'this must be seized by our men within the next three days!' And the command goes out! And our men, hungry, cold and tired to death, are expected to spring into action . . . and sweep everything before them – no matter what the cost."'

F. Farmborough, **Nurse at the Russian Front,** *1974*

In 1917 Russia had two revolutions. The second of these made Russia a Communist country. The first issue we have to study is why Russia had these revolutions in the first place.

The Great War, as people called the First World War at the time, was a big factor in changing people's ideas about their rulers. The war led many people to criticise the people in charge. In the cases of Germany and Russia they overthrew those rulers. In Russia, the ruler was Tsar (Emperor) Nicholas II. He was a dictator and few Russians took the risk of criticising him since it generally meant arrest and a prison sentence, or worse.

Collapse in Russia

When war broke out in August 1914, the people of Russia cheered the Tsar and supported the war. Like the populations in Britain, France and Germany, the Russians felt very patriotic. However, the war went badly for the Russians and nearly two million were killed by the time it ended. By 1916 both the army and the people lost their enthusiasm for a war they were clearly losing. The **morale** of the Russian soldiers collapsed in 1917. Even officers, like the one in Source A, began to criticise their commanders.

Shortages

The war was also causing severe shortages of food and fuel. The food was needed to feed the army and fuel was needed for railway engines and factories. The Russian people went cold and hungry in the bitter winter of 1916–17. By March 1917, they had had enough and protested in the streets, demanding an end to the war and the hunger it had caused. Workers went on strike and joined the demonstrators. Troops sent by the Tsar to crush the demonstrations refused to obey orders and, instead, supported the protests. Once the Tsar realised that the army supported his opponents and not him, he knew he could no longer rule the country and gave up the throne.

SOURCE Ⓑ

Russian women queue for bread during the war. It was hunger like this which forced the civilian population to turn against both the war and the Tsar.

SOURCE Ⓒ

Rasputin was a holy man who was able to ease the suffering of Tsar Nicholas' son, Alexei – possibly by hypnosis. The Tsar's wife, Tsarina, became very attached to Rasputin, convinced that he was sent by God to cure Alexei's illness. Soon there were rumours that she and Rasputin were lovers. Cartoons like this circulated illegally, suggesting that both the Tsar and Tsarina were like little children in the hands of the all-powerful and evil Rasputin., who was now effectively ruling Russia. Rasputin was murdered in December, 1916, by a group of young noblemen. It seems he wasn't an easy man to kill. His assassins first poisoned him, then shot him and finally drowned him in a river before they were sure he was dead.

THINK ABOUT IT

1. What reasons does the artillery officer in Source A give to explain why the men don't want to fight anymore?
2. a) How does the cartoonist in Source C show what Russians thought of the Tsar and Tsarina?
   b) Do you think the cartoonist shared the Russians' hatred of Rasputin?
3. Using the sources and text, write three paragraphs to explain why the people of Russia were turning against the Tsar.
   Think about: how the war affected soldiers; how it affected civilians; the role of Rasputin.

Why did Russia have another revolution?

New government, old mistakes

The 1917 March Revolution led to the overthrow of Tsar Nicholas and the setting up of Russia's first democratic government. Kerensky, the leader of the new government, made the mistake of continuing Russia's involvement in the First World War. This meant the people were still suffering from the same shortages as they were when the Tsar was in charge.

Kerensky hoped that the Russian army would fight with more enthusiasm now that the Tsar had gone, but he was wrong. Soldiers had had enough of the war and, in Lenin's memorable phrase, 'voted with their feet' by simply walking home or seizing trains and ordering the drivers to take them away from the front. Soldiers took their orders not from their officers but from elected assemblies of soldiers, called Soviets. Workers and peasants also elected their own Soviets to represent them.

This allowed a small group of revolutionaries, called Bolsheviks, to gain influence. The Bolsheviks, who later changed their name to Communists, were enthusiastic supporters of the Soviets. The Bolshevik leader, Lenin, wanted a national soviet, representing all the workers, peasants and soldiers to rule Russia, instead of Kerensky's government. The Bolsheviks had been against the war from the start, and now the workers and peasants began to support them against the new government.

SOURCE Ⓐ

'Women can fight. Women have the courage, the endurance and even the strength for fighting. The Russians have demonstrated that and, if necessary, all the other women in the world can demonstrate it.'

Bessie Beatty, an American journalist, writing in 1918 about Russia's Women's Death Battalion – the only group of female combat soldiers in the First World War.

'Peace, Bread, and Land'

Lenin summed up the Bolsheviks' policy in one phrase which their mostly uneducated supporters could easily understand: 'Peace, Bread, and Land.' Ending the war ('peace') would mean the towns and cities could be fed ('bread') and the peasants would then get the land. This would be seized from the rich landowners and given to the peasants, who made up 80% of the population. These policies were very popular and the city council elections for Moscow show just how quickly the people were turning to Lenin. In the elections of June, 1917, the Bolsheviks had won just 11% of the votes, but only three months later they got 51%.

Kerensky's government knew the Bolsheviks were planning another revolution but it was too weak to do anything about it. During the night of November 6 and 7, 1917, the Bolsheviks went into action. Trotsky, Lenin's second in command, ordered the Bolsheviks' armed force, the Red Guards, to arrest Kerensky and his ministers in the Winter Palace.

The Bolshevik Revolution

The government was defended by a few boys, training to be soldiers, and the Women's Death Battalion. Only a few shots were fired in defence of Kerensky's government. Kerensky escaped but the other ministers were arrested. The Bolsheviks had seized power in the capital, Petrograd, without any trouble – though it took a week of fighting for them to get control of Moscow.

Lenin then set up a soviet government of workers, peasants and soldiers for the whole of Russia. Lenin kept some of the promises he had made to the people. In December 1917 the Soviet government signed an armistice with Germany and in March 1918 a full peace treaty was signed. Russia had peace – but only for a few months because soon a civil war would start. The peasants also got their land, as Lenin had promised. But the national soviet never really got to rule Russia. Russia had been a dictatorship under the Tsar and it was now, once again, a dictatorship under the Bolsheviks. It would remain a dictatorship until 1991.

SOURCE Ⓑ

There were about 140 women soldiers in the Death Battalion who were defending Kerensky's government when the Red Guards attacked. They were all taken prisoner and later released.

SOURCE C

The main events of the Russian Revolution, November 1917

THINK ABOUT IT

Revolution!

1. Source C shows a series of illustrations on the events which led to the Bolshevik or Communist revolution in Russia. However, the events are in the wrong order. Do a rough sketch of each of the eight scenes in your book and choose the right caption from Source D for each of them. If you don't like drawing, then just write the captions in the middle of the boxes. Make sure the events are in the right order!

2. Now write a short account of these events in Russia under the title 'Why was there a Communist revolution in Russia?' Each picture and caption should make up one paragraph, so you should have eight paragraphs altogether. Then you must finish with a conclusion. This should explain what you think is the most important reason for the success of Lenin and his Bolsheviks in November 1917.

Try to start each paragraph with a good connecting word or phrase. For example, you should start your essay with the point about how the Russian people showed their support for the Tsar at the beginning of the war. But the next paragraph should be about the huge casualties and how this began to turn the people against the war and the Tsar. A good connecting word to use here is 'However' because it shows the essay is changing direction from support for the Tsar to opposition to him.

The next paragraph should add to the point made in the previous paragraph because it describes how the people were suffering even more hardship caused by the war. Good connecting words or phrases to use here are 'In addition', 'Also', 'Furthermore'.

SOURCE D

a) *Hungry, cold civilians huddled around a stove.*

b) *Dead Russians after a battle*

c) *Hungry, cold civilians huddled around a stove as the shortages continue.*

d) *The Russian people protest against the war, shortages and the Tsar in March 1917.*

e) *Kerensky urges the Russian soldiers to carry on with the war.*

f) *Tsar Nicholas gives up the throne and stops ruling Russia.*

g) *Crowds cheer Tsar Nicholas at the start of the war in 1914.*

h) *Lenin leads the Bolsheviks into revolution to overthrow Kerensky.*

STOP AND REFLECT: In three bullet points, sum up why there was a Communist Revolution in 1917. To do this, choose the three reasons you think were most important.

What kind of war was the Russian Civil War?

A civil war (1918–20) quickly followed the Communist revolution. An anti-Communist army, the Whites, fought against the Red Army to overthrow Lenin's government. To begin with, the Whites wanted to put Tsar Nicholas back on the throne but this became impossible after May 1918. In that month, the Bolsheviks executed the Tsar, his wife, four daughters and young son. Without the Tsar to unite them, the White generals soon began squabbling among themselves and this seriously weakened the White cause. The Bolshevik Red Army, on the other hand, was fully under the control of Trotsky, who proved a very capable commander. When Whites captured Red soldiers they usually executed them. One White journalist witnessed such an execution and he was interviewed for an anti-Bolshevik newspaper, *Der Tag*. The story was published on September 7, 1919.

SOURCE A

'Every soldier is questioned, and if he admits that he is a Communist he is immediately sentenced to death by hanging or shooting. The Reds are well aware of this.

Lieutenant K. approached the captured Red regiment and said: 'Those of you who are true Communists show yourselves courageous and step forward! Slowly in closed ranks over half of the regiment steps forward. They are sentenced to be shot. But before being shot they must dig their own graves.

The condemned are told to take off their clothes. Their uniforms are needed by the Whites. In order to save the clothes from being stained with blood or torn by bullets the prisoners are ordered to undress before they are shot. Slowly the Communists take off their shirts, and, tying their clothes together in a bundle, they put them aside.

They stand there in the field, freezing, and in the moonlight their skin appears extremely white, almost transparent. Each of them is given a pick-axe and they begin digging large common graves. The dew is falling like a mild drizzle and there is a tear in every eye. The naked Communists keep on digging. It is getting darker and darker.

At last the graves have the necessary depth. Lieutenant K. asks them to state their last wish. Two take thin rings off their fingers and give them to the Lieutenant. The others have no wishes to make, although every one of them has a home, a wife, children, relatives. I ask one of them 'Why did you become a Communist?'

He replies: 'Because of this terrible life! The world needs happiness.'

The firing squads are holding their rifles ready to shoot. The naked Communists take their positions close to one another, forming a white wall in the moonlight . . . There is a command, a flash and the sound of rifles . . . The Communists are still standing. A second volley rings out. The bullets strike home in their hearts, thick blood streams leap into space. Some are only slightly wounded. And in the fraction of a second before the soldiers shoot again, I hear deep sickening groans. Volley follows volley. Now those who are still alive cry out: 'Ho there, take better aim!' One points to his heart, crying, 'Aim here!'

Finally, all are dead. Some are lying near the edge of the graves, others have fallen into them. It is all over. Nothing disturbs the quiet.'

From Der Tag, *written by a White journalist, September 7, 1919.*

SOURCE B

White soldiers pose proudly over the bodies of Reds they have just executed.

THINK ABOUT IT

1. The writer of Source A was a supporter of the Whites but the writer seems to feel pity for the Reds. What words and phrases in the source suggest that he feels pity?

2. What qualities do you think the Reds showed in the way they met their deaths? Use the source to support your answer.

3. How does Source B indicate that the event in Source A was not unusual?

4. Re-write Source A as a persuasive text from the point of view of the Reds.

   How would they have reported the story? Make sure you use emotive language with strong adjectives and images to show how cruel, heartless, and pitiless the Whites are.

The civil war was a brutal affair with both sides executing their enemies. Many deaths were not as quick as the ones described in Source A. Eventually, the Reds won – partly because the peasants preferred the Reds to the Whites and partly because of the harsh methods they used against their enemies. Communists learned a valuable lesson during the civil war: arresting, imprisoning and executing your opponents brings results. Joseph Stalin, who followed Lenin as leader of the Soviet Union, was quick to realise this.

STOP AND REFLECT: How does Source A help you to understand why the Reds won the civil war?

How did Stalin change the Soviet Union?

Agriculture

From 1928 onwards Stalin put into operation the plans he had for modernising the country. He forced the peasants to hand over their land and animals to the state in a process called collectivisation. The small farms the peasants had were put together to create large state farms and the peasants were then paid a wage to work on these state farms. Many peasants, especially the better-off ones, called kulaks, were very angry about losing their land (see Source C. About five million peasants died of starvation in the early 1930s – deaths caused by the collectivisation programme.

Industry

Stalin set ambitious targets for each industry in a series of Five Year Plans. These Plans saw a huge increase in Soviet production in key industries, such as steel, coal and oil

However, Stalin didn't bother with increasing the output of **consumer goods**. Workers were forced to live with **rationing** in cramped, very basic accommodation. Exhausted workers who missed their shifts could be punished by having their ration cards taken from them. Nonetheless, by the end of the 1930s, the Soviet Union was second only to the United States as an industrial power.

SOURCE Ⓐ

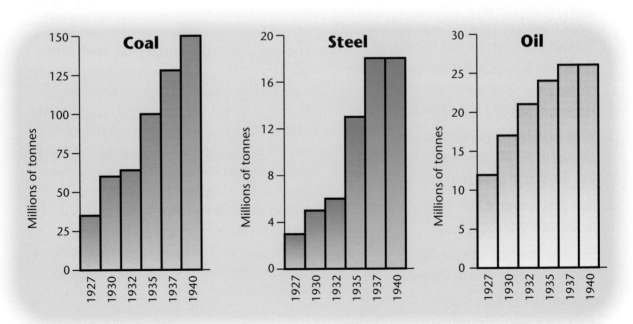

Industrial production during the Five Year Plans which started in 1928. Figures are in millions of tonnes.

SOURCE Ⓑ

The effects of famine on Russian children. About 5 million Russians died in the famine of 1921–2 and about the same number died during the famine of the early 1930s.

SOURCE Ⓒ

The historian, Geoffrey Hosking, describes the collectivisation policy in this source. Viktor Kravchenko was a Communist official who was sent to the countryside to carry out collectivisation.

'The Communist officials searched everything, breaking down doors, tearing up cushions, ripping up floorboards, and confiscated not only food but often furniture, clothes, tools. Many peasants, expecting this, sold their belongings, and slaughtered their cattle for meat. Viktor Kravchenko saw one woman who set fire to her own home. She shrieked at him, "Murderers! We've worked all our lives for our home. You won't have it. The flames shall have it!"…

When he entered a village he was surprised by the complete silence. "All the dogs have been eaten", he was told. "We've eaten everything we could lay our hands on – cats, dogs, mice, birds … the trees have been stripped of their bark, for that too has been eaten."…

Special roadblocks were set up on roads leading into major cities to stop peasants from coming in and begging for bread. When an American worker in Samara saw an old woman and two children lying close to death in the street, a Red Army soldier warned him off, saying, "These people do not want to work. They are kulaks. They are enemies of the Soviet Union."'

Geoffrey Hosking, **A History of the Soviet Union,** *1985.*

THINK ABOUT IT

1. What evidence is there in Source C that many in the countryside were starving?

2. Using Source C, explain why the government could claim that the peasants were to blame for the shortage of food?

3. Look at Source D. Do you think that the artist for this painting witnessed the execution? Read the *provenance* carefully before you answer the question.

4. Do you think that Source D is reliable evidence of Karakhan's execution? You should think about the following:
   - Does the source fit in with what we know about the event?
   - Is there anything in the picture which might be untrue?

The Terror

Stalin was in total control of the country from 1928 onwards. But he was convinced that there were people plotting against him and he was determined to get rid of them in a policy called the Terror. Top of his list were the other important leaders of the Communist Party. From 1936 onwards he put these men on trial and accused them of plotting with Trotsky, who had been forced to leave the country in 1929, and of even plotting with the Nazis! Many confessed that they were guilty in public filmed trials and then they were executed. Some agreed to admit their 'guilt' in order to save their families and some because they were tortured.

Perhaps as many as 3 million 'opponents' were executed during the Terror and another 2 million sent to labour camps where many more died of ill-treatment. Stalin even had the man shot who had organised the killings for him. He wanted everybody to fear that they could be next. Stalin was planning another round of executions when, in 1953, he died.

SOURCE D

*The execution of Lev Karakhan in 1937, on the orders of Stalin. Karakhan, a leading Communist since 1917, had refused to confess and so he was shot in secret, without a trial, in the cellars of the headquarters of the OGPU, the Soviet **secret police**. This painting appeared in an Italian anti-Communist magazine in January, 1938.*

STOP AND REFLECT: Write three sentences entitled: Agriculture, Industry and Terror, each summing up Stalin's impact on Russia.

Pulling it Together

Did the Russian Revolution really make life better for ordinary Russians?

When the Bolsheviks seized control of Russia in 1917 they claimed they were doing it to help the peasants and workers of Russia. Did Communism improve their lives? To answer this question you should look at the evidence and then compare what their lives were like before the Communists took over and after.

Think about:

- Were they better off after the Communist revolution?

- Did they have more freedom after the Communist revolution?

- Some historians have argued that Stalin's policies were harsh but necessary because they made the Soviet Union a superpower which could compete with the United States. You could say whether you agree with this, and why, in your conclusion.

You could start each of your paragraphs like this:

- Historians disagree about … (Say what issues cause disagreements.)

- Some evidence suggests that people weren't better off after the Revolution. People were hungry before the revolution but things got worse after 1917 … (Identify problems after 1917.)

- This is supported by the fact that they had less freedom after the revolution … (Describe ways in which freedom was reduced.)

- On the other hand, there is evidence of improvement …

- Furthermore, some historians point out that Stalin's harsh policies were necessary because … (Again, contrast using positive points.)

- In conclusion, most evidence suggests that … (Make an evaluation. This means coming to a conclusion in which you justify your opinion and say *why* it is better than the alternative.)

CHAPTER 4

American Dream, or Nightmare?

Did the New Deal save America from Depression?

In this chapter you will:

● Examine whether the Depression affected all Americans.
● Consider how the Depression affected one 15-year-old girl.
● Explore how some rich Americans weren't affected at all.
● Decide how successful Roosevelt's New Deal was in ending the Depression.

The 1920s had been good years for most Americans but in the early 1930s an economic **depression** took hold of the United States. This means that a lot of companies went out of business, people lost their jobs, and there was a great deal of hardship as people struggled to feed their families and pay the rent on their homes.

There was no unemployment benefit, so those who had no income or savings were forced to queue for free food. Those who couldn't pay the rent had to leave their homes and live in 'Hoovervilles'. These were crudely built shacks of wood and canvas, on the outskirts of towns and cities. They were called Hoovervilles after the president of the time, Herbert Hoover, because they blamed him for the crisis.

Hoover believed that it wasn't the Republican government's job to provide work and benefits for the poor. If people were given government 'hand-outs', they would get lazy and stop looking for work.

Numbers of the unemployed, in millions, in the United States, 1933–41. The figure for 1933 represents about 25% of the working population.

Most Americans didn't share his attitude. In the 1932 presidential election, 23 million voted for Franklin Delano Roosevelt, the Democratic candidate, compared to 15 million for Hoover. He promised to help the needy and find work for the jobless and this is what most Americans wanted to hear. Roosevelt called his programme the New Deal.

SOURCE Ⓐ

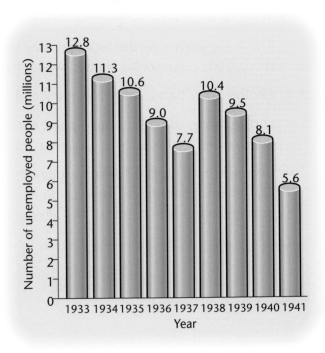

The New Deal

From 1933 onwards, Roosevelt set up the New Deal programme. This included various public works schemes, building roads, hospitals, and airports, or planting trees – just about anything – so that the men involved could be paid a wage. This also meant that they could get out of the poverty they were in and get back some self-respect. They now also had money to spend on goods which meant that factories could start hiring workers again to make these goods.

For those who couldn't get work on these projects, Roosevelt provided some unemployment benefit but, at $15 a week, this was only about half what you could get working on one of the New Deal programmes. The benefit was only paid for four months.

The New Deal did reduce unemployment but it didn't end the Depression. The end of the Depression only happened because the outbreak of the Second World War in Europe meant the Americans began supplying Britain and France with weapons.

There was nothing in the New Deal to help America's black population. This was partly because the New Deal mostly found jobs for skilled workers and few black people had skilled training. Black people complained that the government only did something about unemployment when large numbers of white people began to lose their jobs. Nothing really changed for them in the 1930s. **Segregation** laws still meant they had to live separate lives (see page 52).

SOURCE **B**

A line of black people queuing for government benefits

THINK ABOUT IT

1. Look at Source B. What does the photograph suggest about what happened to black Americans during the Depression?

2. Does this prove that black people were more badly affected by the Depression than white people? Give a reason for your answer.

3. How true, do you think, was the poster's claim that the United States had 'the World's Highest Standard of Living'? Look at Source A to help you.

4. Imagine you are the editor of a magazine for black Americans. Write a commentary of up to 75 words to go with the photograph (Source B), pointing out how your readers might feel differently about the claims in the poster. This is a piece of persuasive writing so it should include strong language showing how the New Deal has failed to help black people. You could use words like 'cheated', 'victimised', 'ignored'.

The Depression: how did poverty affect people's lives?

SOURCE Ⓐ

This interview took place in the late 1960s. The woman interviewed was Peggy Terry. She was about 10 when the Depression started in the United States.

'I first noticed the difference when we'd come home from school in the evening. My mother would send us to the soup line. If you happened to be one of the first ones in line, you didn't get anything but water that was on top. So we'd ask the guy that was ladling out the soup into the buckets – everybody had to bring their own bucket to get the soup – he'd dip the greasy watery stuff off the top. So we'd ask him to please dip down to get some meat and potatoes from the bottom. But he wouldn't do it. We'd say: "Dip down, God damn it …"

My dad said to us kids: "All of you get in the car. I want to take you and show you something … If you think life has been rough for us, I want you to see people that really have it rough." This was in Oklahoma City and he took us to one of the Hoovervilles, and that was the most incredible thing.

Here were all those people living in old, rusted-out car bodies. I mean that was their home. There were people living in shacks made of orange crates. One family with a whole lot of kids were living in a piano box. This wasn't just a little section, this was maybe ten miles wide and ten miles long ….'

[Peggy married when she was 15 in 1935 and hitch-hiked with her husband around America, looking for work.]

I remember one night, we walked for a long time, and we were so tired and hungry, and a wagon came along. There was a Negro family going into town. Of course, they're not allowed to stop and eat in [white] restaurants, so they'd cook their own food and brought it with 'em. They had the back of the wagon filled with hay. We asked if we could lay down and sleep in the wagon and they said yes. We woke up, and it was morning, and she invited us to eat with 'em. She had this box, and she had chicken and biscuits and sweet potatoes and everything in there. It was really wonderful.

I didn't like black people … If they just shipped 'em all out, I don't think it woulda bothered me.'

From **My American Century,** *Studs Terkel, 1997.*

SOURCE Ⓑ

THINK ABOUT IT

It is 1940. You work for a radio station and they have sent you to interview people about how the Depression has affected them. Think of some questions to ask Peggy Terry, based on her account in Source A, and what answers she might give. Try to use the same informal style of language as Peggy. Here is an example of a question to ask her, with the beginning of an answer for you to finish. This activity could also be done in pairs and then acted out in front of the class.

'Peggy Terry is 20 years old. She's been on the road since 1935, with her husband, looking for work.

Interviewer: *Tell our listeners, Peggy, how you managed to eat during the worst days of the Depression.*

Peggy: *It was real tough at first. Mom sent us down to the soup kitchen after school each evening but it wasn't smart to be the first ones in line.*

Interviewer: *Why was that?*

Peggy: *Because ...'*

Here are some examples of other questions you could ask (but you can make up your own):

'Have you come across people worse off than you?' (Source B can help you here).

'Do you feel differently about black people now?'

'Do you think the government has done enough to help America's unemployed?' (Source A on page 50 can help you here).

A Hooverville outside Washington, 1940. A family prepares to cook a meal outside their home

STOP AND REFLECT:
How did the Depression affect the lifestyles of people hit by it?

The Depression: why did people's experiences differ?

Women in the 1930s

The number of women with paid jobs actually went up during the years of the Depression – but only because they were cheaper to employ than men. In 1937 the average annual salary for a woman was $525, compared to $1027 for a man. There was very little in Roosevelt's New Deal to help women. For example, the Civilian Conservation Corps was part of the New Deal programme to find work for the unemployed, in jobs such as strengthening river banks against flooding. It found work for 2.75 million people, but only 8,000 of them were women.

SOURCE Ⓐ

An advertisement from 1938 for holidays flights to Hawaii.

SOURCE Ⓑ

Dr David Rossman was a psychiatrist during the 1930s. His patients were wealthy people. Studs Terkel is a writer who interviews ordinary Americans about their lives in the last century and he interviewed Peggy Terry in the previous pages. He asked Dr Rossman what was going on during the Depression.

'Nothing much. You wouldn't know a depression was going on. Except that people were complaining that they didn't have any jobs. People would work for next to nothing.'

'Your patients, then, weren't really affected?'

'Not very much. They paid fairly reasonable fees. I was making $2000 a month, which was a hell of a lot of money'.

'Did you have any contact with the lower…?'

'The lower classes? Not much. A builder built me a ten-room stone house for $8000. I asked him what he got out of it. He said 'I ate for six months.'

From Hard Times, Studs Terkel, 1970

Businessmen

Powerful businessmen were mostly against Roosevelt's New Deal. They didn't like the way it supported workers by finding jobs for them and paying their wages from taxes. They didn't think it was the government's job to find work for the unemployed and pay them wages, sickness benefit and pensions. Wealthy businessmen thought these policies gave too much power to the government and didn't do enough for their businesses.

Support for Roosevelt

However, not many shared these complaints about the New Deal. In the 1936 election Roosevelt won 61% of the votes as the ordinary people of the United States showed their gratitude to the president for trying to help them. The New Deal didn't end the Depression in America – there were still nearly 10 million out of work in 1939. Only the outbreak of the Second World War finally put Americans back to work. However, most Americans remembered Roosevelt with affection. In 1966 a taxi driver was interviewed for a television programme about Roosevelt. 'He was God in this country,' he said.

THINK ABOUT IT

1. How much did the New Deal do for women?
2. Why were businessmen opposed to the New Deal?
3. What evidence is there in the text that most Americans didn't share their opposition?
4. What do Sources A and B tell you about the impact of the Depression on some Americans?

STOP AND REFLECT: In your opinion what would those opposed to the New Deal have said was the biggest reason for considering it a failure?

Pulling it Together

Did the New Deal save America from Depression?

It is 1941 and you are the editor of an American newspaper opposed to Roosevelt's New Deal. You've decided that there are three key areas where the New Deal has failed:

- It hasn't done anything for black people.
- It hasn't done anything for women.
- It hasn't ended unemployment.

Write three paragraphs, one on each of the points above, under an attention-grabbing headline, such as 'Roosevelt's New Deal flops!'. Make sure that you create a piece of persuasive writing:

- Use active voice (e.g. 'Let's look at the facts').
- Increase the impact by varying sentence length. Explain issues in longer, more complex sentences, and then use short sentences for emphasis.
- Use logical connectives (e.g. 'This shows', 'therefore').
- Set up counter-arguments to demolish them (e.g. 'Roosevelt might claim … but …').
- Use emotive language and value judgements, with forceful adjectives (e.g. 'uncaring') and critical adjectives/nouns (e.g. 'sexist', 'racist').
- Use personal pronouns appealing directly to the reader (e.g. 'we', 'you').

CHAPTER 5

People and War
What was it like to live through 'total war'?

In this chapter you will:

- Decide how effective the bombing of Germany was.
- Plan and present propaganda to use during the London Blitz.

The Second World War is sometimes described as a 'total war'. This means that the entire country, civilians and soldiers, were involved in helping to fight it. Civilians were also directly in the firing line and were made deliberate targets by both sides.

One issue concerning the war which historians have argued about is whether the bombing of Germany by Britain and the United States played an important part in defeating Germany. The man in charge of the Royal Air Force's bombers, Arthur or 'Bomber' Harris, was convinced that bombing raids over German factories would mean that the Germans would not be able to make enough weapons to carry on with the war. Bombing cities would also damage civilian morale.

On the other hand, there was already evidence in 1942 that bombing key industrial targets like factories was unlikely to work. This was because bombing was very inaccurate. One report at the time claimed that only one bomb in four fell within eight kilometres (five miles) of the target. The Americans also used heavy bombing. In October 1943, a huge attack on a ball-bearing factory cut ball-bearing output (essential for engines) by 67%.

SOURCE Ⓐ

'In Berlin the damage was severe enough to cause many to leave the city and to close all schools, but less than half the city's industries stopped work and then for only a short time. Morale did not break in either Berlin or Hamburg. Bomber Command failed to bring German industry to a halt.'

Adapted from **Total War** *by P. Calvocoressi, 1972.*

SOURCE Ⓑ

'On October 14, 1943, 291 US Flying Fortresses set off to attack the greatest centre of German ball-bearing production. The Fortresses did severe damage but 60 were shot down. The strategic bombing offensive brought the German war economy almost to the point of collapse.'

From **World War, 1939–1945,** *by Brigadier Peter Young, 1966.*

SOURCE Ⓒ

'British Bomber Command and the Eighth United States Army Air Force did produce an oil famine in Germany, the collapse of its transport system and terrible destruction of its cities. These results were too late to win the war on their own, but they did make a decisive contribution to the defeat of Germany.'

Adapted from A. N. Frankland, **The Oxford Companion to the Second World War,** *1995.*

THINK ABOUT IT

1. Why did Britain begin its bombing campaign on Germany?

2. Do you think Britain was morally right to bomb deliberately civilians?

3. Sources A –D and the text cover some of the key points about the effectiveness of the British and American bombing of Germany. Your task is to turn these sources and text into a discursive essay in answer to the question: Was the Allied bombing of Germany effective? Start with a sentence about how controversial the argument is with points on both sides and then:

- Those who believe that the bombing was effective and did serious damage to Germany point out that, as Source B says …
- This is supported by the text … and also by Source C.
- Furthermore, the statistics in Source D clearly show that steel and oil production from 1943 to1944 …
- On the other hand, there is evidence to support the opposite view. Source A points out that …
- This opposing argument is strongly supported by a lot of statistical evidence from Source D …
- In conclusion, therefore …

SOURCE D

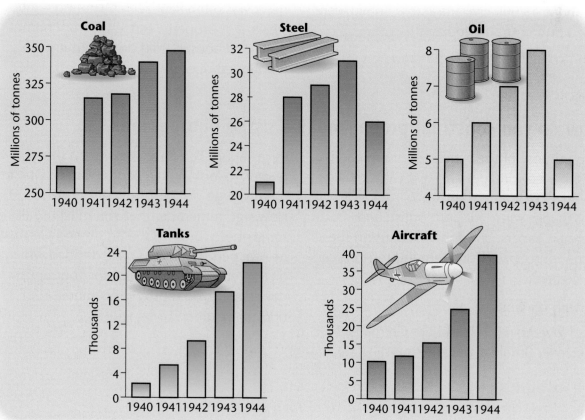

Statistics for German industrial production, 1940–44. The coal, steel, and oil are in tonnes.

How do you construct propaganda?

The Blitz

The term Blitz, from the German word 'Blitzkrieg' meaning 'lightning war', describes the German bombing campaign over Britain's cities from September 1940 to May 1941. The *Luftwaffe* (the German air force) at first bombed airfields and coastal shipping but began bombing cities, with an attack on London, on September 7. This was after the RAF had bombed Berlin on August 24.

The Luftwaffe's raid with 300 bomber planes on September 7 was the beginning of the Blitz. The Germans attacked London every night, and sometimes during the day as well, until the middle of November. From then on the attacks became less frequent. Other cities were also hit – Dover, Glasgow, Swansea, Coventry, among many others. In all about 43,000 civilians across Britain were killed during this period.

Official shelters gave some protection but the most popular shelters were unofficial: the underground stations. These were more likely to be bomb-proof, unlike the official shelters. People began queuing for a place on the platform in the deepest stations, like Hampstead, at 10 am. They were smelly and unhygienic – they only had buckets for toilets -but they were safe. Others chose to leave the cities at night and return in the morning. This was called 'trekking'. Each night 50,000 people 'trekked' out of Plymouth and slept out in barns, cowsheds and even the fields.

In these circumstances, it was vital to keep up public morale so that the population didn't get downhearted. **Censorship** was an important part of keeping up morale, so bad news was often kept secret. Looting – the stealing of property, especially from bomb-damaged houses – did go on but it wasn't mentioned because it was bad for morale.

How do you construct propaganda? – using photographs

The purpose of the activity on these pages is to show how images and text can be used to create **propaganda.** You will act as a newspaper editor for both British and German papers, and show how, using the same sources, very different impressions can be created.

Editing the photos

It is November 1940 and the German air raids over Britain are at their most devastating. You have been given three photos to look at (see pages 60–61). One of them will go on tomorrow's front page. However, remember that you must use the *same* photo for both the British and German newspapers. Once you have decided which picture you're going to use for your British newspaper, you must write a morale-boosting caption to go with it.

THINK ABOUT IT

1. a) With a partner, fill in a copy of the chart below to help you decide which photo to choose. The three photographs are on the next two pages.

   Just jot down ideas at this stage in note form.

   b) Now write out the British caption for the photograph you have chosen. Remember that it must be a morale-boosting one which gives a positive impression of what the picture shows. Limit the caption to a maximum of about fifty words.

   c) Now you have to use the same photograph and write another caption – only this time it must be from a German point of view.

   d) Why do you think your captions (British and German) are examples of effective propaganda? Explain your answer.

2. In March 1943, 173 people, including 62 children, were crushed to death during a stampede to get into Bethnal Green underground station during an air raid alert. The government kept this secret.

   a) Why do you think the government did this?

   b) Do you think the government was right to keep it secret until after the war?

Description of the photograph	Value for British propaganda?	Value for German propaganda?	Is this photo suitable for propaganda?
Photo A: Rescue workers bringing out a victim from a wrecked house.			
Photo B: Londoners sleeping in an underground station.		Britons forced to live like rats; mass mass panic as 'our (i.e. German) glorious air force strikes home'	
Photo C: King George VI and Queen Elizabeth among the rubble of Buckingham Palace.			

Background to the photographs

This information will help you with writing your captions.

Photo A: These rescue workers were just a few of the 1.5 million mostly part-time volunteers who worked in civil defence and Air Raid Precautions (ARP) during the Blitz in the fire service, manning air-raid shelters, emergency kitchens, and in rescue work like this. Rescue work in bombed-damaged buildings was very dangerous as they sometimes collapsed on top of the rescuers.

Photo B: Tube stations provided the kind of safety from German bombs which ground level shelters could not. At first, the government wouldn't allow stations to be used as shelters because it was afraid that Londoners would be too frightened to leave them during the day but the public forced the government to open them at night as shelters.

Photo C: On September 13, 1940, some German bombs fell on Buckingham Palace, damaging some of the outer buildings (though not the Palace itself). At first, the Ministry of Information censored the news and photographs, but Churchill insisted the event be given maximum publicity. The King and Queen were both secretly pleased that the Palace had been bombed because they felt it helped them understand what the ordinary people were going through. 'It makes me feel I can look the East End in the face,' the Queen said.

PHOTO Ⓐ

Rescue workers bringing out a victim from a wrecked house.

PHOTO B

Londoners sleeping in an underground station.

PHOTO C

King George VI and Queen Elizabeth among the rubble of Buckingham Palace

How do you construct propaganda?
– using written sources

SOURCE A

The American ambassador to Britain wrote about the visit of the British Prime Minister, Winston ('Winnie') Churchill, to Bristol after an air raid.

'People were cooking breakfast in half-demolished houses, wherever a stove was working. The Prime Minister arrives and is taken to the most seriously bombed area, leaves his car and starts walking through the streets without guards. Before long, crowds of people flock about him and people call "Good old Winnie", "You'll never let us down"... People were still shaken by the bombing but the whole town was back on its feet again within two hours of his arrival, although no one had got any sleep during the night.'

SOURCE B

A diary entry for September 17, 1940, by Harold Nicholson, a government minister in the Ministry of Information:

'Everybody is worried about the feeling in the East End of London where there is much bitterness. It is said that even the King and Queen were booed the other day when they visited the destroyed areas.'

SOURCE C

A report in the London Evening Standard *during the Blitz describing attacks on railway stations and the courage of the men who repaired them:*

'Stations were hit and trains smashed up before they had left the platforms. Even while the bombs were falling, repair parties were out, working in the dark or by the light of searchlights on some damaged portion of a line that had to be repaired. They worked all night, suffering many casualties but they stuck at it until the job was completed.'

SOURCE D

An American journalist, Ben Robertson, wrote this account for his magazine in the US about London after one air raid:

'We made a tour of a southeast suburb where a church and houses had been demolished during the night ... A crowd of people had assembled, and a woman pushing a baby-carriage said to us: "It will take a million bombs to get London down."

Everywhere there are craters and ruin, but the city in this crisis has found a new spirit. Everywhere there is courage and six million people who had lived ordinary lives are now learning what it is like to live in defence of civilisation.'

Source	Positive points	Negative points	Use / edit / bin
A	Enthusiasm for PM; …	References to 'half-demolished houses'; [add further negative points]	Mostly suitable. Edit out …
B			
C	Courage of railway workers; 'worked all night'; …		Edit out …
D			

THINK ABOUT IT

Read Sources A–D opposite. As editor you have to decide which of the following sources are suitable for inclusion in your newspaper. You can decide to use the whole source as it is, change some of it or reject the source altogether. Once again, you must record your decisions on the chart above.

STOP AND REFLECT:
Why should historians be cautious about using evidence put together in time of war? Explain how 'propaganda' can make evidence difficult to trust.

Pulling it Together

What was it like to live through 'total war'?

Each of the points below should be the focus for each of five paragraphs.

- Define 'Total War'. Use words which introduce a topic (e.g. 'A phrase to describe modern war is …') Use explanatory connectives (e.g. 'This means …') Or set up a question in order to explain it (e.g. 'What does this mean?').

- Explain how and why civilians became front-line targets for enemy bombers. Open the paragraph with explanatory words (e.g. 'Total War made civilians targets because …').

- Describe what life was like under air attack. Use powerful descriptive words (e.g. 'horror', 'defenceless', 'mounds of rubble').

- Contrast this with how propaganda tried to keep up civilian morale. Signal the start of this paragraph with contrasting connective words (e.g. 'However …' 'Despite this, governments tried to …').

CHAPTER 6

The Jewish Tragedy

How did the war change Nazi treatment of the Jews?

In this chapter you will:

- Investigate how the Nazis treated the Jews in the early stages of the war.
- Learn what the Final Solution was.
- Discover what life was like in the camps.
- Examine how the Holocaust happened.

'The Jewish Question'

Hitler had persecuted Jews from the moment he took control of Germany (see page 24), but this persecution didn't often lead to their deaths and in the early stages of the Second World War, Hitler's policy towards Europe's Jews was confused. The 3 million Jews of Poland, for example, were sent to live in **ghettos**. Conditions were so bad that between 1939 and 1941 perhaps as many as 600,000 of Poland's Jews died in these ghettos and camps. It seems, though, that even as late as June 1941, the Nazi leaders were still not sure just what solution they had in mind for the 'Jewish Question'. Some said the Jews should be put to work, others that they should all be left to die in the ghettos. The German invasion of Russia in that month forced them to make up their minds.

A group of Jewish men, women and children, stands at the edge of a pit, waiting to be shot. One of the children takes a last look at the horror behind her.

SOURCE Ⓐ

Sometime during the autumn of 1941, Hitler decided that all of Russia's 5 million Jews, and any others in German hands, would have to die. This seems to have been for one of two reasons. Firstly, for Hitler, the invasion of the USSR was a 'life or death' struggle between Nazis and Jews and Communists. Secondly, as it became clear in late 1941 that Germany might *not* beat the USSR, the Nazis finally decided to totally destroy the people they hated the most – the Jews. Hitler told Himmler, head of the **SS**, to find a way of doing it. Clearly, execution by rifle fire was too slow and messy (see Source B). It would not be long before Himmler came up with a solution.

SOURCE Ⓑ

'Without weeping or crying these people stood together in family groups, embracing each other and saying goodbye ... An old woman with snow-white hair held a one-year-old child in her arms, singing to it and tickling it. The child squeaked with delight. The married couple looked on with tears in their eyes. The father held the ten-year-old boy by the hand speaking softly to him. The boy was struggling to hold back his tears. The father pointed a finger to the sky and stroked his head and seemed to be explaining something to him ... I can still remember how a girl, slender and dark, pointed at herself as she went past me saying 'twenty three'.

I walked round the mound and stood in front of the huge grave ... I estimate that it already held about a thousand bodies. I turned my eyes towards the man doing the shooting. He was an SS man; he sat, legs swinging, on the edge of the ditch. He had an automatic rifle resting on his knees and was smoking a cigarette. The people, completely naked, climbed down steps which had been cut into the clay wall of the ditch, stumbled over the heads of those lying there and stopped at the spot indicated by the SS man. They lay down on top of the dead or wounded; some stroked those still living and spoke quietly to them. Then I heard a series of rifle shots. I looked into the ditch and saw the bodies contorting or, the heads already motionless, sinking on the corpses beneath. Blood flowed from the napes of their necks.

I am making the above statement in Wiesbaden, Germany on 10 November 1945. I swear to God that it is the whole truth.'

A German engineer's eye-witness account of a massacre of Jews in the Ukraine, in October 1942

THINK ABOUT IT

1. What is so remarkable about Source B is the absence of emotive language in the way this shocking scene is described. It is hard to be sure how the German engineer felt about what he saw. Rewrite the second paragraph using more emotive language which clearly gets across a sense of shock, horror, and outrage.

2. The German, Hermann Graebe, who witnessed the killings in Source B was a civilian engineer, not a soldier. He noted the event in his diary but made no protest. Do you think people who witness shocking events but don't try to stop them are also partly to blame?

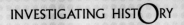

What was the final solution?

The Wannsee Conference, 1942

The Nazis had already made a start by 1942 on what has become known as the Holocaust. The Holocaust was the campaign of persecution and murder of Europe's Jews by the Nazi government . During the first two years of the war, this meant mass-executions of men, women and children by firing squads. But these killings were slow and messy. At the beginning of 1942 the Nazis decided on a new policy of murder.

In January 1942, a group of leading Nazis met at Wannsee, just outside Berlin. Here leading Nazis, such as Reinhard Heydrich and Adolf Eichmann, discussed a new, more organised policy of mass-murder. They described this policy as the Final Solution. The Wannsee Conference, which lasted only 90 minutes, did not start the Holocaust. That was already taking place. By this time Germany controlled a huge area of Europe in which the vast majority of Europe's Jews lived. This made their mass-murder much easier and it could also be done in secret, far away from the view of the Allies.

Death factories

In early 1942 the SS set up the first death camps in Poland. The Jews arrived by train in trucks normally used for cattle. The SS target was to gas the victims within two hours. For things to go as smoothly as possible it was vital that there were no scenes of panic or chaos. The victims had to be unaware of what was going to happen to them.

SOURCE A

'At last, after thirty-two minutes, they are all dead …The dead stand like pillars pressed together in the chambers. There is no room to fall or even to lean over. Even in death one can tell which are the families. They are holding hands in death and it is difficult to tear them apart in order to empty the chambers for the next batch. The corpses are thrown out with sweat and urine, smeared with excrement and menstrual blood on their legs. The corpses of children fly through the air. There is no time …Two dozen dentists open the mouths and look for gold … Some of the workers check genitals and anus for gold, diamonds and valuables.'

An eye-witness account of a gassing by an SS officer, Kurt Gerstein, in August 1942, at Belzec.

The mathematics of murder

Treblinka could 'process' (another SS term for murder) 1,000 prisoners an hour. The SS worked a 12-hour shift. Auschwitz was the first camp to use Zyklon B. This gas came in cyanide crystal form. The crystals were sprinkled into the gas chamber through openings in the roof. The five chambers at Auschwitz could 'process' 2,000 at a time. The heat from the bodies packed into the chamber helped the crystals give off a poisonous vapour which caused death by suffocation within ten minutes. The chamber was then ventilated so a squad of prisoners could enter. The bodies were searched for hidden valuables and gold teeth were removed with pliers. Then they were taken to the ovens where they were burned.

SOURCE B

This drawing is titled 'Selection for Gas Chambers'. It was drawn by David Olere, a prisoner who was saved because his artistic talents were useful to the SS. He wrote and illustrated their letters and he worked in the gas chambers at Auschwitz clearing the bodies out.

THINK ABOUT IT

1. What was the Final Solution?

2. Why did the Nazis tell the Jews that they were going for a shower?

3. When the Nazis discussed the Holocaust in writing they always used terms like 'special treatment', 're-settlement', 'processing' rather than gassing or killing. Why do you think they did this?

4. The SS officer who witnessed the scene in Source A shot himself after writing this account in 1945. Is there anything in the language in the source which suggests how he felt about what he had witnessed?

STOP AND REFLECT: In what way was the policy of the Final Solution different from how the Nazis treated Jews in the early years of the war?

What was life like in the death camps?

The selection

Some camps, like Auschwitz, had two roles. They were killing centres and they were work camps. When the cattle trucks arrived at the camp, the SS made a 'selection'. The SS commander checked the new arrivals as they filed past him. Those who looked over 15 and appeared strong and healthy were sent to the left. The old, the sick, pregnant women, and women with young children were all sent to the right. On average about 10% of a **transport** would be sent to the left. These were called 'work-Jews.' The rest made their way directly to their deaths in the gas chambers.

Those who had passed the selection could expect to live for about three months. That is how long the SS calculated people could survive on the rations they gave them. Every time a new transport arrived, the SS made another selection of the 'work-Jews'. Those who looked sick and weak were killed to make way for a new batch of 'work-Jews.' Diseases like **typhus** also killed large numbers because of the crowded conditions.

SOURCE A

'Here is a woman – she walks quickly, but tries to appear calm. A small child with a pink cherub's face runs after her, and, unable to keep up, stretches out his little arms and cries: "Mama! Mama!".

"Pick up your child, woman!"

"It's not mine, sir, not mine!" she shouts hysterically, covering her face with her hands. She wants to hide, she wants to reach those who will not ride the trucks, those who will walk on foot, those who will stay alive … She wants to live.'

One prisoner describes how a woman behaved when she realised that women with young children would be gassed; quoted in This Way for the Gas, Ladies and Gentlemen, *by Tadeusz Borowski. Borowski was a young Pole, born in the Soviet Union, but not a Jew, so he was given the job of getting the Jews off the trains and prepared for the selection. He killed himself in 1951, out of a sense of guilt over his role in the camps.*

SOURCE B

'I will never forget a woman, I believe her name was Kleinova, who always used to carry her bread ration around with her, so that she would not die of hunger. One day her bread ration fell into the dirty toilet and out of sheer despair she crept into the pit, or it seems that she had let herself fall into it, to get her bread ration. Though she, and the bread, were disgustingly filthy, this was of no importance to her. The animal instinct to survive, by keeping food at hand, had won.'

Judith was a 13-year-old Jewish girl when she was transported with her parents to Birkenau camp. This is taken from Memories of My Childhood *by Judith Jaegerman, 1985.*

SOURCE ⓒ

This is one of the drawings made by Zofja Rozenstrauch, a Polish prisoner in Auschwitz from 1943–5. They were used as evidence in the trial of one of the Nazi leaders, Adolf Eichmann, in 1961.

Food

In theory the daily food ration for a prisoner in a work camp was made up of 350 grams of bread, and half a litre of substitute coffee for breakfast. Lunch and supper was a litre of potato and turnip soup. Four times a week the soup was supposed to contain 20 grams of meat. In practice, workers never got anything like this.

You had to be cunning if you wanted to live for longer than the usual three months. It wasn't a good idea to be at the front of the queue for soup. Those at the front got the soup from the top of the cauldron. This was always thin and watery. The closer to the bottom your helping was, the better the chance it might contain some potato or turnip. Prisoners in work groups sometimes had the chance to smuggle in food from outside, but the punishment was severe as Source C shows. Neither was it sensible to be too fussy about what you ate, as Source B makes clear.

THINK ABOUT IT

1. Why do you think typhus was so common in these camps?

2. Why did the woman in Source A pretend that the child wasn't her son?

3. Why is this source so shocking?

4. In what different ways do Sources A, B, and C show life in the camps?

5. Do you think Borowski, the author of Source A, should have been punished as a criminal for his role in the camp?

6. There are still some very old people alive today who took part in the killing of Jews and who have not been put on trial. Do you think it too late to bring these people to justice?

STOP AND REFLECT: Which one of the three sources on these pages best sums up the horror of life in the camps? In pairs make a decision. Then share your opinion with the class. Let others comment on what they think about your ideas and reasons.

What were conditions like in the death camps?

Dying conditions

There were separate barracks for men and women but conditions in them were much the same. There were also separate sections for the different types of prisoners. Jews had the worst conditions and the worst food. Political prisoners, such as Communists, were normally better off. All prisoners wore a prison uniform which was made of cheap, flimsy material and soon became a dirty, smelly rag. Each prisoner had a bowl and a pair of wooden clogs.

SOURCE Ⓐ

Each morning the prisoners had to stand outside the barracks in their uniforms for hours at a time while the SS guards did a roll-call to see who had died during the night and to make sure there had been no escapes. Roll-calls, particularly in the freezing weather, often led to the deaths of the sick. Punishments were always done in public to set an example to the prisoners (See Source B).

The sleeping accommodation was in levels of bunks. The bunks were nothing more than planks of wood with gaps between them. There were no mattresses. The best level to sleep on was the top. Those on the lower levels had to deal with the problem of urine and diarrhoea dripping onto them from the bunk above.

This painting by David Olere shows the scene inside a gas chamber as the gas takes effect.

SOURCE B

'The three victims mounted together onto the chairs. The three necks were placed at the same moment within the nooses. 'Long live liberty!' cried the two adults.

But the child was silent.

"Where is God? Where is He?" someone behind me asked.

At a sign from the head of the camp, the three chairs tipped over ...

Then the march past began. The two adults were no longer alive. Their tongues hung swollen, blue-tinged. But the third rope was still moving; being so light, the child was still alive ...

For more than half an hour he stayed there, struggling between life and death, dying in slow agony under our eyes. And we had to look him full in the face. He was still alive when I passed in front of him. His tongue was still red, his eyes were not yet glazed.

Behind me, I heard the same man asking:

"Where is God now?"

And I heard a voice within me answer him:

"Where is He? Here He is – He is hanging here on this gallows ..."

That night the soup tasted of corpses.'

From Elie Wiesel, Night, *1982. As a 15-year-old, Wiesel was imprisoned in Auschwitz with his father.*

SOURCE C

'It was common practice to remove the skin from dead prisoners. It was chemically treated and placed in the sun to dry. After that it was cut into various sizes for use as saddles, riding breeches, gloves, house slippers and ladies' handbags. Tattooed skin was especially valued by SS men ... Also we frequently got requests for the skulls or skeletons of prisoners. In this case we boiled the skull or the body ... The SS men would say "We will try to get you some with good teeth."'

An account of by Dr Franz Blaha, one of seven doctors who carried out medical experiments at Dachau concentration camp.

THINK ABOUT IT

1. How did experiences of the Holocaust, like those in Source B, affect how some people thought about God?

2. What effect do you think the public execution described in Source B would have had on the other prisoners? Think about:
   ● The horror of watching it.
   ● The fear of it happening to them felt by other prisoners.
   ● The effect this might have on any plans to escape.

STOP AND REFLECT: In a short paragraph explain how the Nazis used cruelty to break the spirit of prisoners.

Pulling it Together

How did the war change Nazi treatment of the Jews?

In the 1930s the Nazis treated Jews terribly. But it was during the War that this accelerated into mass murder.

You are now going to answer this key question. The chart on these pages provides ideas to help you. Write an essay with an introduction, four paragraphs and a conclusion. The themes for each paragraph are provided below.

Introduction: 'The Holocaust happened during the Second World War for many reasons. These include ...' List possible reasons but do not go into detail yet.

Paragraph 1: Use Point 1 in the chart here. Make sure you explain how the fact that anti-Semitism had been around for so long made it easier for Hitler to get support for his wartime acceleration of racial murder.

Paragraph 2: Use Point 2 here. You need to explain that Nazi propaganda against the Jews started gradually so that Germans became used to it, even before the war.

Paragraph 3: Use Point 3 here. The chaos caused by the war made it harder for the Allies to stop the Holocaust. Also the invasion of the USSR led to a new stage in mass murder.

Paragraph 4: Explain how the Nazis were able to carry out such a mass murder of millions of people.

Conclusion: Finish your essay by bringing the evidence together to answer the question. Explain what you think was the most important reason why the cruel treatment of the Jews turned into mass murder during the Second World War.

1. **Anti-Semitism** in Germany and Europe had existed for centuries.

Martin Luther was a German monk. His views on Jews here, written in 1543, were shared by many Christians.

'The Jews are nothing but thieves and robbers and everything which they eat or wear has been stolen from us. Thus they live from day to day, together with wife and child, by theft and robbery. We let them get rich on our sweat and blood, while we remain poor and they suck the marrow from our bones. What shall we Christians do with this rejected and condemned people, the Jews?

First, set fire to their synagogues [places of worship] or schools and bury and cover with dirt whatever will not burn. Second, I advise that their houses also be destroyed.'

From **Luther's Works,** *Volume 47:* **The Christian in Society IV.**

4. New technology – gas chambers.

2. Nazi propaganda against the Jews

How did cruel treatment turn into mass murder?

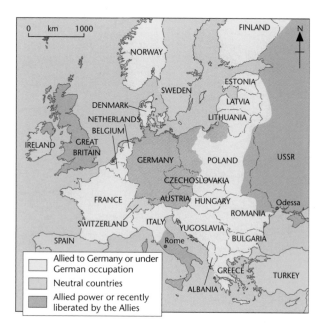

3. Even in early 1944 Germany still controlled a vast area of Europe.

CHAPTER 7

The World Divided

Why was there a Cold War after the Second World War?

In this chapter you will:

- Examine why there was a Cold War after the Second World War.
- Investigate why the Cold War got colder.
- Learn about the death of a young Berliner who tried to cross the Berlin Wall.
- Put yourself in the place of President Kennedy during the Cuban Missiles crisis.
- Explore how the Cold War ended.

Why did a 'Cold War' start?

SOURCE Ⓐ   *Differences between Communism and Capitalism*

Living standards are low but everyone has a job and there is less of a difference between rich and poor.

Living standards are much higher but there is a bigger difference between rich and poor people.

The origins of the Cold War between the United States and the Soviet Union go back to 1917 when the Communists in Russia carried out a successful revolution (see Chapter 3). The United States and the rest of Europe, however, believed in Capitalism (see Source A) and democracy. From then on, Communism was feared and hated in the West, especially in the United States. (See Source A for the differences between Communism and democracy).

Churchill and Truman (who became president of the USA in 1945 when Roosevelt died) suspected that Stalin, the leader of the Soviet Union, was trying to spread Soviet Communism across the world. Stalin suspected that Churchill and Truman were looking for ways to destroy Communism. Now that the Americans had a terrible new weapon – the atomic bomb – they had the power to do it. Relations between the old allies became frosty; the cold war had started.

Europe after 1945

Stalin decided that Russia needed to be protected from invasion by creating a ring of friendly, Communist countries around it.

One by one, these countries, already occupied by the Soviet army during the war, became Communist. By the end of 1948 Poland, Czechoslovakia, Hungary, Romania, Bulgaria, East Germany, and Albania all had Communist governments. Yugoslavia was also Communist but it was not under Soviet control. West Germany and the other countries of Europe had democratic governments, supported by the United States.

In 1946, Churchill used the phrase 'the Iron Curtain' to describe the division between the Communist half of Europe in the East and the democratic half in the West. The 'iron' part of the curtain was the barbed wire fence, which now kept each side apart.

SOURCE **B** *Europe in 1949.*

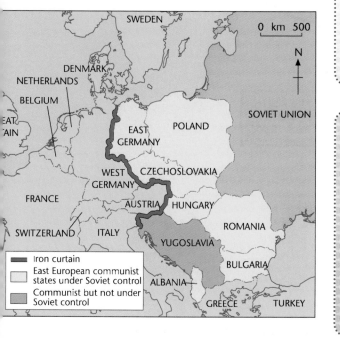

Iron curtain
East European communist states under Soviet control
Communist but not under Soviet control

THINK ABOUT IT

Looking at the map of Europe in 1949, why might Stalin be:
a) pleased,   b) displeased with what he saw?

STOP AND REFLECT: Who was more to blame for the tension after 1945: the USSR or the United States?
Write three sentences:
Why each side feared the other.
How the US felt about the Soviet Union spreading its influence across Eastern Europe.
How the Soviet Union felt about the US having the atomic bomb

How did the Cold War get colder?

Divided Germany

Germany was a special problem for the Soviet Union and the West. The western part of Germany was controlled by Britain, France and the United States while the eastern part was controlled by the Russians. Berlin, the capital of Germany, was divided in exactly the same way but it was deep inside the Soviet zone (see Source A).

In 1948 Stalin decided that he wanted to control all of Berlin and not just its eastern half. Since Berlin was inside the Soviet zone of Germany, it was an easy matter to shut off all road and rail routes into West Berlin. In this way, the Western powers would be forced to give up West Berlin and the Russians would occupy it. Instead, the Americans, British, and French brought food and fuel supplies to the city by air ('the Berlin Airlift') for thirteen months.

Eventually, Stalin realised he couldn't starve West Berlin and gave up. He re-opened the rail and road routes to the city in 1949. Stalin was aware that the Soviet Union was a long way behind the United States in nuclear technology (the Russians didn't have their own nuclear bomb until August 1949) and so couldn't risk a war.

SOURCE Ⓐ

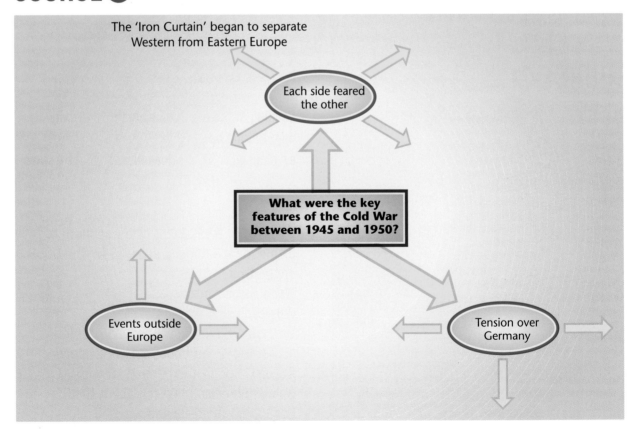

The key features of the Cold War 1945–50.

The Cold War goes global

There was some good news for Stalin, though, at the end of the decade. In 1949 the Soviet Union developed its own atomic bomb, and in October of that year China's Communists finally took control of the country after two decades of war. Now the country with the biggest population in the world was also Communist. However, a plan to spread Communism elsewhere in South East Asia didn't go according to plan. The invasion of South Korea by communist North Korea led to the Korean War (1950–3) but the invaders were defeated, mainly because the United States sent 400,000 troops to defend South Korea.

In 1965 the United States began sending troops to South Vietnam in an unsuccessful attempt to stop communist North Vietnam from taking over the South. The Americans were convinced that Communism was gradually taking over the whole of South East Asia and it had to be stopped.

THINK ABOUT IT

1. The information below shows key features and events of the Cold War between 1945 and 1950. Decide which information from it should go by each of the three areas on Source A. Do this as a discussion in small groups. One has already been filled in for you (*The 'Iron Curtain' began to separate Western from Eastern Europe* has already been put in the section *Each side feared the other* in Source A).

2. Use the information from the completed Source A to write three factual paragraphs about the Cold War. Use the information to explain: why each side feared the other; how events outside Europe made things worse; tension over Germany. Explain how each event in each category caused the issue you are writing about.

Events and Key Features of the Cold War

- United States used the first atomic bomb, 1945
- Berlin and Germany divided between the West and the Soviet Union
- The 'Iron Curtain' began to separate Western from Eastern Europe
- Soviet Union took control of Eastern Europe
- West Berlin cut off by Stalin, 1948–9
- Berlin Airlift, 1948–9
- Soviet Union developed its own atomic bomb, 1949
- Communists took power in China, 1949
- Korean War broke out, 1950

STOP AND REFLECT: Why were the United States and the Soviet Union so afraid of each other? Explain in a paragraph, summing up what you have learned here.

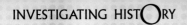
Why was the 'Wall' such a deadly place?

During the 1950s relations between the United States and the Soviet Union got better, got worse, and then got better again. Relations improved because Stalin died in 1953 and the man who took over as leader of the Soviet Union, Nikita Khrushchev, wanted better relations with the West. In 1956 he made a speech to Soviet Communists. He astonished them by telling them of the terrible crimes which Stalin had committed during the Terror of the 1930s. Khrushchev also said that the USSR should learn to live with the West in peace. In 1959 the Soviet leader even visited the United States as part of this 'thaw' in relations between the two countries. The visit went well but Khrushchev, for some strange reason, wasn't allowed to visit Disneyland!

However, despite this apparent 'thaw', in 1961 the Cold War suddenly got colder. The main reason for this was the building of the Berlin Wall in 1961.

In 1961 the Communist government of East Germany decided that too many young and skilled East Germans were leaving the country for life in the West by walking into West Berlin. With Russian approval, the Communist government in East Germany built a wall around the whole of West Berlin so that there could be no further escapes. This wall literally divided families in two. Relatives in East Berlin couldn't visit their families in the western part of the city. At least a hundred East Berliners lost their lives trying to cross the Wall. Peter Fechter was the fiftieth.

SOURCE A

'Peter Fechter was an 18-year-old bricklayer who lived in East Berlin. He wanted to live in the west of the city with his sister. The only problem was the Wall, which stood between him and her. Together with his friend, Helmut Kulbeik, he worked out an escape plan using an empty building.

They checked out the building on August 15, 1962. They could get in without being seen and found a window which hadn't been completely boarded up. This would be their escape route. They knew full well this was a deadly business. In the year since the wall had gone up, 49 East Berliners had died trying to cross over to the West.

Two days later they returned. They pulled away the boards which partly blocked up the window and then Peter climbed through and dropped to the ground, followed by Helmut. The two lads raced across the open space towards the wall. Helmut was the first to start climbing over the wall, ignoring the barbed wire which tore and tugged at his clothes. As he was about to drop down to the other side and freedom he realised Peter was still at the foot of the wall – too terrified to move.

Then the firing began. Peter was hit in the back by several bullets as he at last tried to climb the wall. He got to the top but couldn't get any further and then he fell backwards. He lay at the foot of the wall, on the wrong, East German side. One of the bullets had pierced his lung.

Peter lay there calling for help, as his blood spilled out onto the concrete floor. By now a crowd of West Berliners had gathered on their side of the wall. They had seen everything. They called on the East German guards to help him but they stood still, keeping their rifles pointed at the youth. The Americans troops on their side of the wall were ordered not help. "This is not our problem", one of them said.

After fifty minutes the East German guards carried Peter's body away on a stretcher. During those fifty minutes he had slowly bled to death.'

Adapted from www.swlink.net

SOURCE B

Peter Fechter's body at the foot of the Wall – on the East German side.

THINK ABOUT IT

The story of Peter Fechter's death is a good example of a recount text but your task now is to write a persuasion text. Here you need to influence what people think by using forceful language which doesn't show both sides of the argument. Instead, it should describe how terrible the Wall is and how cruelly the East German guards have behaved. Since you're writing this article the day after the event for an American newspaper, there are a couple of sentences you need to remove from the recount. Which ones are they and why? Rewrite the story as a persuasion text. You might want to think about using some of the following words or others like them: *daring*; *heartless*; *evil*; *angry*; *desperate*; *murder*; *tragedy*.

STOP AND REFLECT: Why do you think the building of the Wall made relations between the Soviet Union and the USA worse?

79

Why did the 'Cuban missiles crisis' occur?

SOURCE Ⓐ

The Bay of Pigs incident

Relations became even more icy in 1962. In this year the world came the closest ever to a Third World War. In 1959 Fidel Castro led a successful revolution against the dictator of Cuba. The Americans immediately acted against Castro. They accused him of being a Communist and working for the Russians. The Americans were worried because Cuba was only 150 km (90 miles) from the American coast.

The US Central Intelligence Agency (CIA) came up with a plan to overthrow Castro using a force of 1,500 anti-Castro Cubans which would invade Cuba. The invasion force landed at the Bay of Pigs in April 1961. It was a total flop. Castro, fearing another invasion, asked the Soviet leader, Khrushchev, to set up nuclear missiles in Cuba.

In October 1961, the Americans discovered the existance of these missiles in Cuba. President Kennedy decided to force the Soviet Union to remove them – and he succeeded. But for thirteen days the world faced the possibility of a nuclear war in what became the Cuban Missiles Crises.

Soviet cargo ship 'Kasimov' carrying Ilyushin 28 bomber planes in 'kit' form on board. The long rectangular crates contain the fuselages or central sections of the bombers. The Ilyushin 28 has a range of 2400 km.

THINK ABOUT IT

You work for the US Central Intelligence Agency and have just been handed Sources A, B and C. Your task is to analyse them and prepare a report for President Kennedy as to what they mean. The chart opposite will provide you with the basic information.
In your report:
● Provide Kennedy with all the information he will need about what the sources show.
● Indicate how serious these developments are for the United States' safety.
● Suggest possible strategies to follow and *their possible consequences.*

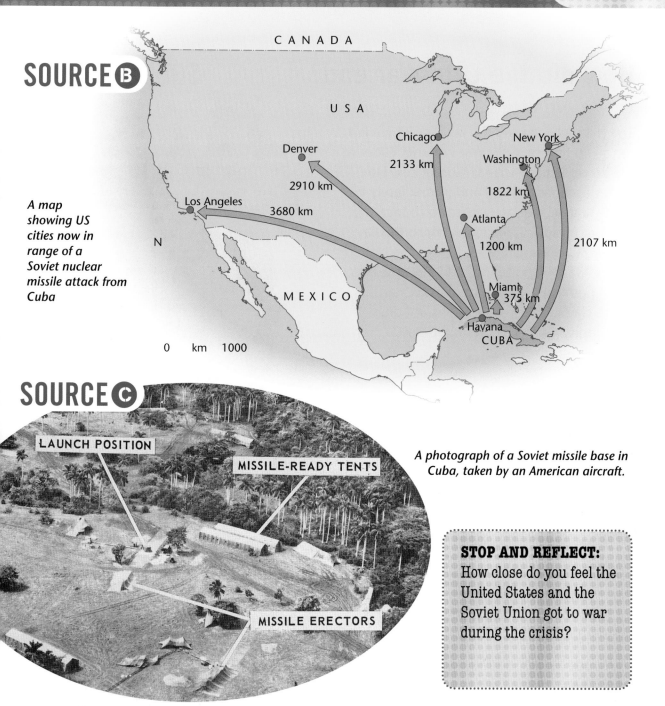

SOURCE B

A map showing US cities now in range of a Soviet nuclear missile attack from Cuba

CANADA

USA

Denver

Chicago
2133 km

New York

Washington
1822 km

2910 km

Los Angeles
3680 km

Atlanta
1200 km

2107 km

N

MEXICO

Miami
375 km

Havana
CUBA

0   km   1000

SOURCE C

LAUNCH POSITION

MISSILE-READY TENTS

MISSILE ERECTORS

A photograph of a Soviet missile base in Cuba, taken by an American aircraft.

STOP AND REFLECT:
How close do you feel the United States and the Soviet Union got to war during the crisis?

Source	What it shows	How serious is it?	What to do about it?
A	Soviet cargo ship 'Kasimov' carrying Ilyushin 28 bombers in 'kit' form on board. The long rectangular crates contain the fuselages or central sections of the bombers. The Ilyushin 28 has a range of 2400 km.	The Ilyushin 28 is a bomber but it doesn't carry nuclear bombs. Many of our cities are within its range …	We could: • Sink the ship or ships carrying weapons to Cuba. • Tell Khrushchev to send his ships back or we'll sink them. • Put our navy between the ships and Cuba and stop them that way.
B	US cities in range of a Soviet missile attack from Cuba.	These medium range missiles can reach targets 2400 km away. There are also missiles in Cuba with a 4000-km-range.	We could: • Bomb these sites. • Threaten to bomb if Khrushchev doesn't remove the missiles. • Wait to see if Khrushchev agrees to withdraw his ships.
C	Soviet missile base at San Cristobal in Cuba.		

How did the Cold War end?

The man who started the process which led to the end of the Cold War was the leader of the Soviet Union: Mikhail Gorbachev. He became leader in 1985 and immediately he made it clear that he wanted to reduce the number of nuclear weapons which Russia had. Ronald Reagan, President of the United States, was willing to listen. In December 1987 both men agreed to get rid of an entire class of nuclear weapons: medium-range missiles. This represented 3,800 nuclear warheads.

The end of Communism

Gorbachev encouraged Russians to criticise the Communist system so that improvements could be made. He hoped that improving people's lives and changing the system would make Communism work better. Unfortunately for Gorbachev, he started a process which he later found he could not stop. People weren't happy with changing the Communist system to make it work better – they wanted to get rid of it altogether.

In August 1991, Communist army leaders tried to overthrow Gorbachev and put a stop to the changes he had introduced. Gorbachev was arrested but the plot failed when units of the Russian army fought off the Communist troops. Gorbachev was free but the people didn't want him or his 'improved' Communist system. By the end of 1991 Gorbachev was out of power and Communism was finished. The United States, or rather democracy and capitalism, had 'won' the Cold War.

SOURCE Ⓐ

An American cartoon, published in 1970, comments on the Strategic Arms Limitation Talks (SALT) between the Soviet Union (left) and the United States (right). The purpose of the talks was to persuade both sides to cut the number of their nuclear weapons.

SOURCE Ⓑ

'Eduard Shevarnadze [the Soviet Foreign Minster under Gorbachev] reckoned that as much as 50% of the Soviet Union's national income was spent on defence, arms, and the armed forces, depriving the Soviet people of a better life. In the United States spending on national defence ran at over 10% of national income in the 1950s and 6% in the 1980s.'

From The Cold War, *by Jeremy Isaacs and Taylor Downing, 1998.*

SOURCE ☉

'The winter before August 1991, food shortages brought the Russians to the point of total desperation. The following winter, things were even worse. At one point there was no milk. When there was milk, there was no meat. For a while there were no sanitary towels, no tomatoes, no shoes. When there was fruit juice, there was no toilet paper. When there were cigarettes, there was no soap. Factories closed because there was no heat. Communism turned out to be the worst economic disaster in the history of the world … Until recently, everything was always sold at a loss. A loaf of bread used to cost 20 kopeks to buy but 60 kopeks to bake.'

Jeffrey Robinson, **The End of the American Century,** *1997.*

THINK ABOUT IT

1. Look at Source A. What does it suggest about relations between the United States and the Soviet Union?

2. How far did relations change between the two countries by December 1987?

3. How far does Source B back up the point made in Source A? Explain why.

4. What does Source C suggest about the quality of life of the people of the Soviet Union under the Communist system?

Pulling it Together

Why was there a Cold War after the Second World War?

Imagine you could interview the last leader of the Communist USSR.

Get into pairs. One of you is the interviewer and the other is Gorbachev. The interviewer should prepare questions to ask Gorbachev.

- 'Who do you think was to blame for starting the Cold War?'
  Gorbachev may refer to the threat of America's atomic bomb. You could counter this with a question about the Soviet take-over of Eastern Europe.

- 'Why did the Soviet Union nearly start a nuclear war over Cuba in 1962?'
  Gorbachev might argue that the Soviet Union was merely defending Cuba from another US attack. How would you reply?

- 'Why is the Cold War over now?'
  If Gorbachev is honest he will say it is because the Soviet Union couldn't afford to keep up with US nuclear weapons spending.

- 'Do you regret the changes you started in the 1980s?'
  Gorbachev's policies in the mid-1980s started changes which led to the end of Communism in the Soviet Union and his place as leader. Does he regret this?

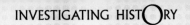

CHAPTER 8

Complex Conflicts

What has been the role of religion, politics, and money in causing recent conflicts?

In this chapter you will:

- Explore why Yugoslavia was torn apart.
- Discover some of the factors behind the attacks on the World Trade Center, 2001.
- Note some of the complex reasons behind modern conflicts.

Religion has played an important part in conflict in the twentieth century, especially after 1945. Religious differences led to the deaths of perhaps a million Indians as Hindus, Muslims, and Sikhs fought each other after India became independent from Britain in 1947. Hindu India and Muslim Pakistan are still arguing over who should control the region of Kashmir.

Religious conflict has scarred Europe as well. Tension in Northern Ireland between two groups of Christians – Catholics and Protestants – has led to the deaths of over 3,000 people since 1969. However, while some forms of religion may provide a spark that sets off conflict, it is usually mixed in with other causes. In Northern Ireland, for example, there are political differences over whether Northern Ireland should be British (and Protestant) or part of the Catholic Irish Republic. In the Middle East, tension between some Arab states and the West is partly caused by oil. Some people in the Middle East suspect that Western countries, like the United States, are trying to control the Middle East to make sure they receive vital oil supplies. In their view the US supports Israel in the region against the mostly Muslim Palestinians to make sure there is at least one Middle-Eastern country to support the US in the event of a war over oil. Some Americans argue that they support Israel because it is the only truly democratic country in the Middle East. Some enemies of Israel, they claim, also want to take over the country. There is also the question of whether the Jews are entitled to a country of their own, especially after the events of the Holocaust. Controversy continues to surround Israel's occupation of lands that the Palestinians claim as their own.

Like any important aspect of life, it is vital to remember that different people have different approaches to religious beliefs.

SOURCE Ⓐ

Map of the ethnic divisions of Yugoslavia in the early 1990s.

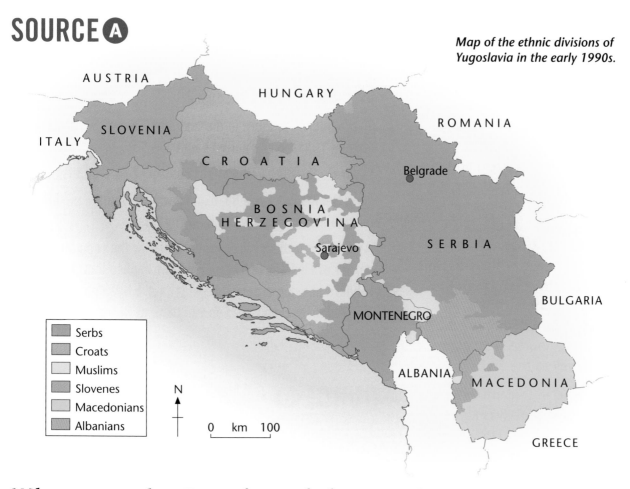

Legend:
- Serbs
- Croats
- Muslims
- Slovenes
- Macedonians
- Albanians

N

0   km   100

What was the Bosnian nightmare?

The biggest conflict in Europe since the Second World War took place in the 1990s in Yugoslavia, but here again religion was only one of the reasons for the distrust between communities.

Yugoslavia came into existence in 1919 after the First World War, as part of the Treaty of Versailles. After the Second World War it became a communist **republic** under the strong leadership of Joseph Tito. It then consisted of six smaller republics (Slovenia, Croatia, Serbia, Bosnia-Herzegovina, Montenegro and Macedonia) linked to a central government in Belgrade, the capital. After Tito's death in 1980, however, the republic gradually began to fall apart as separate groups, such as the Slovenes and Croats, wanted their own states.

Slovenia, Croatia, and Macedonia became independent states in 1991, and Serbia and Montenegro joined together in 1992 to become Yugoslavia. That left only Bosnia-Herzegovina. This was the most difficult area because it consisted of three different religious groups: Muslims, who made up 44% of the population, Orthodox Christians (Serbs) who were 31%, and Catholics (Croats) who were 17%.

Each group tried to gain control with the result that civil war broke out in Bosnia in 1992, with the better-equipped Serbs winning most of the battles.

It has been claimed that the Serbs brutally terrorised Muslim and Croat civilians to leave their areas so the Serbs could take over. Rape and murder have been cited as methods used. Perhaps 200,000 men, women and children were killed in the Bosnian civil war, most of them Muslims. At first, Muslims and Croats co-operated against the Serbs, but between February 1993 and March 1994 Croats and Muslims started fighting each other (see Source A on page 87) as well as the Serbs.

Eventually, in December 1994 a cease-fire was agreed but the Serbs, who now controlled 70% of Bosnia, refused to give up any territory. **NATO** air-strikes on the Serbs in 1995 forced them to accept a peace settlement which gave 51% of Bosnia to the Muslims and Croats, and 49% to the Serbs.

STOP AND REFLECT:
Look at the map on page 85. Even if the three sides in Bosnia had agreed to divide peacefully the area between them in 1992, why would this still have been very difficult to achieve?

THINK ABOUT IT

1. Why was the future of Bosnia likely to cause the biggest problem for Europe in the 1990s?

2. What evidence is there in the text that Tito was essential to keeping Yugoslavia a united country?

3. Why were the Serbs able to get control of 70% of Bosnia?

4. Using the map on page 85, explain why Slovenia was able to become independent without any fighting?

5. Some of the ordinary men responsible for the rape and murder of civilians in Bosnia gave the excuse that they were 'soldiers obeying orders' who would have been punished if they had disobeyed. What do you think of this point of view?

SOURCE B *A Muslim soldier mourns at the graveside of his friend in a military cemetery in Bosnia in 1994.*

Why were people used as bombs at Novi Travnik?

THINK ABOUT IT

Anthony Loyd, the author of Source A, was a British journalist who reported on the war in Bosnia. Is there any evidence that he was sympathetic to one side or the other? Think about:

- What he chose to write about – did Loyd have a reason for writing about this incident?
- Use of language, e.g. adjectives or phrases which suggest sympathy for the Muslims or hostility to the Croats.
- The impact on the reader – what does it make you feel?

SOURCE A

This source describes the terrible deaths in 1993 of three Muslim soldiers outside the town of Novi Travnik in Bosnia.

'"Don't shoot, don't shoot", the three soldiers cried out to their comrades as they staggered up the rain-soaked slope towards the Muslim soldiers at the edge of Novi Travnik. The men approaching them were their own, captured days earlier by the Croats. Now, forced back across no man's land, the prisoners lurched unnaturally up the hillside. Their hands were strapped to their waists. Explosives were attached to their chests, linked to the Croat positions by coils of wire that unravelled slowly with each step they took. The human bombs were returning home.

As the distance narrowed a Muslim officer shouted at his men to shoot them. They refused. Two of the prisoners were from the Novi Travnik, pre-war friends of the men in the trenches. The Muslim troops argued frantically among themselves. Some of the men ran back from their trench to their bunkers. The officer was screaming at the three men to halt. They kept on walking. As they neared the edge of the trench he too fell back. There were three individual explosions, so close together as to roll into one thunderous roar. Blood, fragments of metal, and human tissue sprayed through the trees.

For a few seconds there was silence. A couple of soldiers and the officer peered over the edge of the trench. Before them they could make out three pairs of legs. It was all that was left of their friends.'

Adapted from My War Gone By, I Miss It So, *by Anthony Loyd, 1999.*

STOP AND REFLECT: What does this incident tell you about why the civil war in Bosnia was such a brutal one?

Why did Admira and Bosko die?

Admira Ismic and Bosko Brkic were two 25-year-old students from Sarajevo in Bosnia. They had been together for nine years. When the civil war in Bosnia broke out in 1992, Bosko, a Christian Serb, decided to stay behind in Sarajevo with Admira, his Muslim girlfriend. Relationships and marriages between Muslims, Serbs and Croats were common in Bosnia – especially in Sarajevo – before the civil war.

During 1993 the Serb army surrounded Sarajevo. Life became very dangerous for those in the Muslim sections of the city as Serbs regularly fired into them. In May 1993 they both decided that they would try to escape from Sarajevo and make a new life for themselves.

To escape, they would have to cross 'no man's land', a bridge between the Serb and Muslim-controlled areas. Snipers on both sides shot and killed those who tried to cross the bridge but some did get through. Friends in the Muslim army promised that their snipers would not fire on them.

Together they began running as fast as they could across the bridge. They had almost made it across when a sniper's bullet shot Bosko dead. He crumpled to the ground. Admira was also hit but she dragged herself back to her boyfriend and placed an arm around him before she too died.

Each side blamed the other for their deaths and no one would risk going out into 'no-man's-land' to get the bodies. Instead, they lay there for eight days, huddled together, before the Serbs recovered their bodies during the night and buried them.

When the war broke out in 1992, Admira's mother was asked whether the war and the hatred it caused would ever end the love affair between her daughter and Bosko. 'Only a bullet could separate them', she had replied.

'Only a bullet could separate them' – the bodies of Bosko Brkic and Admira Ismic lie together in 'no-man's-land' between Serb and Muslim lines in Sarajevo, May 1993. Three years later they were reburied – together – in a Muslim cemetery.

SOURCE (A)

STOP AND REFLECT:
How does this story support the idea that civil wars are often more terrible and tragic than 'normal' wars between different countries? Think about how: 'normal' wars are usually between the armed forces of different countries; there are internationally agreed rules about how these wars are fought; ways in which civil wars are different.

SOURCE **B**

Front-page outline.

Newspaper Date

NEWSPAPER TITLE

Interview with one of the friends of Bosko or Admira

Possible questions:

How do young people feel about this war?

Do you think that couples with different religions can ever be happy together in Bosnia?

Do you see any way of ending this war?

LEAD STORY HEADLINE

Write your caption here

BACKGROUND TO THE CRISIS IN BOSNIA: HOW DID IT ALL START?

THINK ABOUT IT

This tragic, moving story captured the attention of the world's press in May 1993. Your task is to re-create the event as a front-page newspaper story. Source B provides some ideas of how to cover it. The world's press, at the time, treated it as a Sarajevo 'Romeo and Juliet' story because it was about two lovers whose love for each other ended in tragedy – as in Shakespeare's play.

Decide what the style of your page will be. Remember that different papers have different styles and readership. *'Broadsheets'* concentrate more on the details and on depth of analysis and use more complex sentences and vocabulary. *'Tabloids'* tend to focus more on 'human interest' and use less complex sentences and vocabulary.

- If it is a broadsheet front-page, like in the *The Times* or *The Independent*, then give more space to the background material about the crisis and less on the story of the young lovers
- If it is a front-page from a tabloid, like the *The Sun* or *The Daily Mirror*, then concentrate on the tragedy of the young lovers.
- You might also want to discuss which side might have been the ones to shoot the two young people.

What is the 'New Terrorism'?

Terrorism is the use of violence to achieve political aims. Terrorists usually represent such a small section of the population that their ideas don't get enough support for them to succeed peacefully, so they use violence instead. Very small and deadly terrorist groups sprang up in Italy and Germany in the 1970s. They used terrorism to try to bring about revolutions in their countries, but failed because hardly anyone shared their aims. This is not true for Osama bin Laden.

Osama bin Laden

Towards the end of the twentieth century a new type of terrorism came about. This new terrorism was based on religious belief. For the vast majority of Muslims, Islam is a peaceful religion but extremists, such as Osama bin Laden, have used Islam to gain support for their aims. Osama bin Laden grew up in a very wealthy family in Saudi Arabia but he left all this in the early 1980s to fight the Russians in Afghanistan. Here the Soviet Union was the enemy after it invaded the Islamic country in 1979. The United States also saw the Soviet Union as its enemy and provided Afghan freedom fighters with weapons and money to fight the Russians. Once the Russians were defeated, bin Laden, and his *al-Qaeda* (which means 'the Base') organisation began their campaign against the United States.

Bin Laden established a clear programme. First of all, to get rid of American influence in the Middle East. Saudi Arabia has in the past, allowed US troops in its country and the

Americans provide vital support for Israel. Bin Laden also opposed America's policy against Iraq. As well as ending American influence in the area, he established another target: to get rid of the governments of countries such as Saudi Arabia and Egypt, the leaders of these countries, in bin Laden's opinion, not being true followers of Islam. Al-Qaeda was to overthrow their leaders and make Egypt and Saudi Arabia into what he called 'proper' Islamic countries.

Why terrorism?

The big problem for al-Qaeda was finding a way to end US influence in the Middle East. This is where terrorism came in. The terrorist strategy of bombing American targets and killing US citizens all over the world aimed to make the Americans withdraw from the Middle East. The alternative situation al-Qaeda hoped for was that that the Americans would become so enraged by these killings that they would launch military attacks on one or more Islamic countries to hit back at the terrorists. This, al-Qaeda hoped, would create massive support for the organisation from angry Muslims across the world.

This is where the events of September 11, 2001 have great significance. This devastating, spectacular attack on the United States, in which over 3,000 innocent people were killed, was designed to provoke the United States into a military assault on Islam.

THINK ABOUT IT

1. Why is it possible that bin Laden and the US at one time could have co-operated with each other?

2. Why have the rulers of Egypt and Saudi Arabia also had reason to fear bin Laden?

3. Al-Qaeda set out two strategies to weaken the power of the United States. Explain these strategies.

STOP AND REFLECT: Why is new terrorism more dangerous than the terrorist groups of the 1970s? Mention: money; suicide volunteers; use of advanced communication methods (such as satellite phones, the Internet); popularity of ideas for some people.

In 1998 al-Qaeda blew up the US embassies in Kenya and Tanzania, killing 224 people. These are the ruins of the embassy in Tanzania.

SOURCE Ⓐ

What does the September 11 attack tell us about a divided world?

On the morning of September 11, 2001, 19 terrorists hijacked four American passenger jets. The hijackers took control of the aircraft and changed direction. These men, who had trained as pilots in the United States, flew two of the aircraft straight into the twin towers of the World Trade Center in New York (see Source A). The WTC was a big business center and the towers were the tallest buildings in New York.

A third plane, with 64 people on board, was flown by the terrorists into the Pentagon building in Washington, the headquarters of the American military at 9.43 am. Here about 200 people died, including those on the plane. About 25 minutes later, at about 10.10 am, another hijacked plane crashed into a field in Somerset County, Pennsylvania, not far from Washington. It is probable that in this plane, United Airlines Flight 93, some of the 38 passengers fought with the hijackers to prevent them from crashing the aircraft into their target – possibly the White House, where the president of the United States resides.

The passengers on Flight 93 knew what had happened to the other three hi-jacked aircraft after phoning relatives from the plane. A group of men decided 'to do something'. The mother of one of these men later said, 'It gives me a great deal of comfort to know that my son may have been able to stop the killing of many, many innocent people.'

Around 2,800 people died in both the towers of the World Trade Center. Of these people, 479 were from the emergency services who had gone into the towers to help get people out before they collapsed. Another 157 were on the planes. Each plane was carrying more than 90,000 litres of fuel and it was the heat from the explosion of the fuel which caused the towers to collapse. The south tower was hit more than 15 minutes after the north tower but it collapsed first because of the greater weight of the number of floors above it.

Only four people survived from the floors above the point where the two planes hit the towers. Of those trapped above the flames, about 200 chose to jump the 350 metres or so to their deaths, rather than be burnt alive. No trace of 1,500 of those who died was ever found.

THINK ABOUT IT

1. Why do you think the terrorists chose as their targets:
   a) the World Trade Center
   b) the Pentagon
   c) possibly the White House?

2. Why do you think many people criticised America's security services after the attacks?

3. Osama bin Laden probably had two aims in carrying out the attacks:
   - attracting the attention of the world to his organisation
   - provoking the United States into attacks against Islamic countries.
   Which of these aims posed the greatest threat to world peace, in your opinion?

SOURCE Ⓐ

① 8:45 Eastern Standard Time
American Airlines flight 11, a Boeing 767 with 92 people on board is flown into the north tower.

② 9:03 Eastern Standard Time
United Airlines flight 175, a Boeing 757 with 64 people on board is flown into the south tower.

③ Evacuation of both towers and the surrounding area continues as the emergency services move in. Debris rains down onto the streets below.

④ 10:00 Eastern Standard Time
The south tower collapses in a huge cloud of dust and debris.

⑤ 10:28 Eastern Standard Time
The north tower collapses.

The attacks on the World Trade Center.

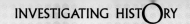

Pulling it Together

Where do we go from here?

At the beginning of the book you were asked whether you were optimistic about developments in the twenty-first century. It is now time to think about this question again. Will the twenty-first century be a safer, fairer and better one to live in than the twentieth century?

Think about:

- Where the major causes of conflict remain today (e.g. Middle East, Kashmir).

- Which conflicts of the twentieth century *seem* to have been ended (e.g. Northern Ireland, Bosnia).

- Whether terrorism can be stopped.

- Whether the poorer countries of the world might get a fairer share of the world's wealth.

You could structure your answer like this:

There are still many places in the world today where there is conflict caused by religion, politics and money …

The most serious of these conflicts is in the Middle East because it involves …

However, it seems that some of the last century's conflicts have ended …

Nonetheless, we are still faced by the terrible problem caused by worldwide terrorism …

Some people argue that if the world were a fairer place, there would be less conflict. For example …

In conclusion, I am **optimistic** / **pessimistic** about the twenty-first century because ….

GLOSSARY

anti-semitism the hatred and persecution of Jews

armistice an agreement between two sides in a war to stop fighting

boycott a boycott happens when people refuse to buy goods from a particular shop or business, in this case Jewish ones

censorship the policy of preventing the public from getting information the government wants to keep secret

Cold War the state of tension (but without actual fighting) between the United States and the Soviet Union which lasted until 1991

colony a country ruled by another, more powerful country

Communist someone who believes that the workers should take control of the government and share out the wealth of the rich among themselves

conscription the policy of making men enlist in the armed forces

consumer goods goods which make people's lives easier and more comfortable, such as washing machines, refrigerators, radios and clothes

democracy a way of running a country in which the government is chosen by the people

depression a situation in which there is high unemployment and many businesses go out of business

desertion running away from the fighting; the usual punishment for this was death by firing squad

dictator a ruler with total control over how a country is governed. A country ruled by a dictator is called a dictatorship

empire a group of colonies under the rule of another country

Fascist someone who is against democracy and believes in rule by one powerful leader, supported by a strong military to attack weaker countries

ghetto a small, sealed-off section of a town or city in which Jews were forced to love

hyper-inflation this happens when prices rise so fast that money becomes worthless

morale during a war, good morale means the soldiers are willing to go on fighting and want to win

NATO the North Atlantic Treaty Organisation: a military alliance of 19 countries, including the United States and Britain

no-man's-land the land between two opposing sides which neither one controls

optimist someone who feels good about a situation or the future

pacifist someone who is against wars and refuses to fight in them

patriot someone who supports their country, especially against its enemies

pessimist someone who feels bad about a situation or the future

propaganda persuading people to believe something, often by telling them lies

provenance the background information to a source providing details such as the author, date and place of publication

rationing limiting the amount and type of foods people can buy in times of shortage

republic a country which does not have a king or queen

revolution the overthrow of a country's ruler or government, often using violence

secret police police who deal with people who oppose the government rather than criminals by arresting, torturing and sometimes executing them

segregation the policy of keeping black and white Americans apart by giving them separate facilities such as hotels, and schools

SS originally Hitler's personal bodyguard, its members were the most fanatical and loyal to Hitler

transport a Nazi term used to describe a group of arrivals, usually by train, at a camp

typhus a disease spread by fleas and body lice which leads to severe pain, fever and eventually the failure of vital organs such as the heart and kidneys. It spreads easily from person to person

Index